# Words of Life

## THE BIBLE DAY BY DAY
## WITH THE SALVATION ARMY

### EASTER EDITION  JANUARY-APRIL 2003

Hodder & Stoughton
LONDON SYDNEY AUCKLAND
AND THE SALVATION ARMY

British Library Cataloguing in Publication Data
A record for this book is available from the British Library

ISBN 0 340 78654 X

Printed and bound in Great Britain by
Bookmarque

Hodder & Stoughton
A Division of Hodder Headline Ltd
338 Euston Road
London NW1 3BH
www.madaboutbooks.com

# DANCING IN THE RAIN

After months of drought
and the prospect of a long gasping summer
the rain came
gentle silent persistent
not stopping for a whole day
every tree weeping with joy
cobwebs sparkling with diamond drops
the world washed clean

That was the day
war began in Afghanistan
the first bombs dropped on an evil terror
that was the day
an immigrant taxi–driver was bashed to death
that was the day
a neighbour's child was bullied and beaten
in the school playground

God, the world is weeping
with bombs and bashing and bullying
yet your cross proclaims the Easter resurrection
surrounded by death you call us to live
in a world crazy with hatred
you draw us into your song of love
in a parched and weary land
you invite us to join you
dancing in the rain.

*Barbara Sampson*
*New Zealand*

# CONTENTS

Major Barbara Sampson writes...

# MAJOR BARBARA SAMPSON WRITES...

Even before the events of 11 September 2001, I had decided that this Easter edition of *Words of Life* would deal with some of the tough questions, such as:

• Why is prayer hard at times?
• Why do dreams die?
• Why does God sometimes lead us by a roundabout way?

Then it happened, a terrible, senseless act which, as so many people have said, changed the world – our world – for ever. But it is because of another event that changed the world – every generation's world – for ever, that this edition has been able to be written.

Easter is the closest we get to God's answers to life's tough questions. The cross on which Jesus died is, in the words of T. S. Eliot, 'the still point in a turning world'. In a turning, tipping world of terrorism and tragedy, the cross speaks of love that will never let us go. It speaks of hope that will never surrender to despair. It speaks of light that will never be exting-uished. It speaks of life – resurrection life – that has conquered death for ever.

As we walk this Easter journey together, may we find some answers to our tough questions, and discover that, even on the bleakest, darkest day, God is with us.

# ABBREVIATIONS USED

| | |
|---|---|
| J. B. Phillips | *The New Testament in Modern English*, J. B. Phillips, Geoffrey Bles, 1958. |
| *The Message* | *The Message: The New Testament Psalms and Proverbs*, Eugene H. Peterson, NavPress, 1993, 1994, 1995. Scripture taken from *The Message*. Copyright © by Eugene H. Peterson, 1993, 1994, 1995. Used by permission of NavPress Publishing Group. |
| NIV | New International Version |
| NRSV | New Revised Standard Version |
| SASB | *The Song Book of The Salvation Army*, 1986 |

# JOSEPH THE DREAM CHASER

## Introduction

What could be better for the January holidays than a rollicking good story? Joseph fits the bill perfectly.

Joseph's story begins in the book of Genesis when he is seventeen years old. He has a most unpromising beginning as his father's favourite, a spoiled brat, to put it frankly. His story ends thirteen chapters and almost 100 years later, when he is 110 years old, an age of great honour for a man of great stature. In the course of his story we see the full range of human passions: political intrigue and sibling rivalry, love and hate, jealousy, lust, ambition, heroism and mercy.

In Jewish tradition Joseph is called *tzaddik*, Joseph 'the Just'. His whole life reflected the justice and righteousness of God. He resisted temptation, he kept his word, he waited with patience, he administered God's justice, he extended God's mercy to those who did not deserve it. Joseph may be the hero, but the major player in this story is God.

Before he died, Jacob, Joseph's father, prayed a blessing on each of his sons. The blessing he gave to Joseph was that he might be a fruitful vine, and a prince among his brothers (*Gen 49:22,26*). As we read on beyond the end of the book of Genesis, we discover that these blessings did come true, and in a way that could only be explained in God-terms.

In Joseph's story, perhaps more than in any other biblical narrative, we discover that, 'Even where no man could imagine it, God had all the strings in his hand' (Gerhard von Rad).

# WEDNESDAY 1 JANUARY
## Joseph Introduced

### Genesis 37:1–4

'Now Israel loved Joseph more than any of his other sons,
because he had been born to him in his old age; and he made
a richly ornamented robe for him' (v. 3, NIV).

The book of Genesis is a book of beginnings. It tells the beginnings of the heavens and the earth, of light and darkness, of land and vegetation, of animals and human beings, of sin and redemption. Above all it tells the beginnings of relationships – between God and nature, God and people, and people with people. It tells of God initiating and making covenants with his chosen people, pledging his love and faithfulness to them and calling for their allegiance.

Genesis is divided into ten major accounts that tell the story from Adam, through Abraham to Isaac, Jacob and Joseph. The narrative concerning Jacob and Joseph is an integral part of this patriarchal history, for it is through Joseph that the covenant family in Canaan becomes an emerging nation in Egypt. Joseph's is a story of deliverance against all odds, in which God delivers his people Israel into Egypt and then out of Egypt, eventually to carry the message of deliverance and redemption to all the nations of the world.

This grand narrative begins, rather surprisingly, with a young man of seventeen who can only be described as a spoiled brat. Jacob had settled in Canaan, the land that his father Isaac had claimed as home (35:27–29). Along with his brothers, Joseph's work was to shepherd the flocks. Although not Jacob's youngest son, Joseph was born to Jacob in his old age and was his father's favourite, probably because he was the son of Rachel, the wife whom Jacob had loved most dearly.

For whatever reason, either some dark flaw of character, or simply because he was a typical seventeen-year-old, Joseph told tales to his father about the behaviour of his older brothers, thus incurring their hatred. To make matters worse, Jacob made Joseph a richly ornamented robe that set him in a class apart, exempting him from the menial tasks of farming. Not surprisingly, his brothers were disgusted at such favouritism. Joseph may be God's chosen person but he could hardly make a worse first impression.

### To reflect on
*With such a beginning, we wonder where this story will end!*

# THURSDAY 2 JANUARY
## Joseph in Dreamland

Genesis 37:5–20

'His brothers were jealous of him, but his father kept
the matter in mind' (v. 11, NIV).

To spoiled brat and telltale, now add braggart. Joseph should have known better. He should have recognised his brothers' hostility, seen it in their eyes, heard it in their snide remarks. But he didn't. With a mixture of exuberance and folly, he took his opportunity one day, perhaps while they were all having breakfast, to tell his latest dream. 'We were out in the field gathering wheat when suddenly my bundle stood up and all of yours formed a circle around mine and bowed down to it.' Joseph's grandiose ideas did nothing to endear him to his brothers. 'What!' they retorted. 'You wish to reign over us?'

Then it happened again, a dream in which the sun, moon and eleven stars were bowing down to him. This time the inference was even more pointed. Even his father reacted when Joseph told him this dream. 'Do you really think that your mother and I (the sun and moon) and your brothers (the eleven stars) are going to bow down to you?' Jacob had already bowed down before his brother (33:3). Must he now bow down before his son as well? Jacob 'kept the matter in mind', no doubt wondering if such a dream was a pointer to some divine destiny. He was not unlike Mary, the mother of Jesus, who pondered the deep questions of exactly who her son might be (*Luke 2:19,51*).

For the brothers, resentment mixed together with hatred and jealousy had produced a very nasty brew. That murderous mix spilled over one day when the brothers were out in a distant area around Dothan, shepherding the flocks. They saw Joseph, 'that dreamer' (literally, 'master of dreams'), coming towards them, on a mission from his father to check up on them. It took only a few moments to form a plan. 'Let's kill him, dispose of his body and tell Father that a wild animal devoured him.'

The brothers were blinded by their desire to get rid of the mischief-maker and his dreams, but they would discover that real God-given dreams cannot be disposed of quite so easily.

3

# FRIDAY 3 JANUARY
## Joseph in the Pit

Genesis 37:21–36

'So when Joseph came to his brothers, they stripped him of his robe – the richly ornamented robe he was wearing – and they took him and threw him into the cistern' (vv. 23,24, NIV).

When Joseph reached his brothers, they grabbed him. Thanks to eldest brother Reuben's intervention, they did not kill Joseph outright, but tore off his ornamented coat and threw him into a pit. Reuben had it in mind to rescue him later, but the plot changed when Judah spotted a passing caravan of Midianite traders and persuaded his brothers to sell Joseph into slavery. A later reference (42:21) suggests that Joseph cried out for mercy, but these verses report no pleading, no bargaining. Just silence, like a sheep about to be slaughtered.

What was going on in Joseph's mind as he felt the dark sides of the dried-out cistern? Did it occur to him that his father might be behind all this? After all, his father had sent him to check up on his brothers (v. 14). Did the far-distant memory of Mount Moriah and of Abraham binding Isaac sweep over Joseph? Was his father Jacob trying to match the heroic faith of his grandfather Abraham? Was Joseph, as his father's favourite, now being offered as a sacrifice? The terror of such a possibility may have been even greater than the terror of being at the mercy of his brothers.

Both incidents, Moriah and Dothan, speak of the providence of God. Both began in terror and ended in a miracle. Isaac was saved by the sudden appearance of a ram (22:13); Joseph by a passing caravan. On another day, generations later than Joseph, another son was led like a lamb to slaughter. This one too was silent, as a sheep before her shearers (Isa 53:7), but this Lamb was slain so that all the world might be saved.

With Joseph out of the way, the brothers returned to their father, carrying Joseph's coat covered in blood. Jacob could come to no other conclusion but that a wild beast had killed his son. This man, who once deceived his father Isaac (27:35), was now deceived by his own sons. His guilt and grief almost destroyed him. He cried out, 'I will wear my mourning clothes until I die.' And he nearly did.

# SATURDAY 4 JANUARY
## Joseph in Egypt

Genesis 39:1–6

'The LORD was with Joseph and he prospered, and he lived in the house of his Egyptian master' (v. 2, NIV).

As Joseph disappeared into the shimmering heat and blinding sandstorms of the desert, back home his father wept for his lost son. Suspense is now added to Joseph's story as a dark incident concerning his brother Judah is inserted into the narrative.

Joseph had been separated from his brothers by force, but Judah voluntarily broke away from the family in order to seek his fortune among the Canaanites. His story is a sordid mix of disaster and dishonouring, bereavement, animosity, superstition and prostitution. Judah's immorality revealed here stands in sharp contrast to the moral character of Joseph, shown in the next chapter. As we read this chapter, however, we do well to remember that Judah's child Perez, born illegitimately and in such scandalous circumstances to his daughter-in-law Tamar, became the head of the leading clan in Judah, the ancestor of David and ultimately of Jesus. God, at times, uses the most unlikely means to further his purposes!

Joseph arrived in Egypt and, to begin with, everything went well. The Midianite traders sold him to Potiphar, an Egyptian who was one of Pharaoh's officials. Joseph's work in Potiphar's house was appreciated and he was given more and more responsibility. A refrain sang its lilting tune over him, like piped music in a shopping mall today. 'The LORD was with Joseph . . . the LORD gave him success in everything he did . . . the LORD blessed the household of the Egyptian because of Joseph.' His success could only be explained as God's *shalom* – blessing, favour, prosperity and peace – which overflowed from Joseph to those whom he served. In no time, it seemed, he was made estate manager, in charge of all Potiphar's business affairs.

The boastful youngster from Canaan seems to have grown in stature since we first met him. Here he is, trustworthy, competent, and well-built and handsome into the bargain. He sounds like a great new find for the front cover of the *Egyptian Ego*. But Joseph will discover all too soon that God's overflowing blessing does not make him immune to trouble and testing.

# SUNDAY 5 JANUARY
## A Prayer for Shalom

Psalm 72:1–17

'Endow the king with your justice, O God, the royal son
with your righteousness' (v. 1, NIV).

In ancient Israel, the king stood between God and his people. He passed God's blessing along to them and he passed their needs on to God. In this psalm, as the king is about to be crowned, the people pray God's blessing upon him, knowing that blessing for him will mean blessing for them also. With confidence they name the blessings they seek – justice, righteousness, prosperity, in a word *shalom*, peace, salvation and well-being. Their prayer is big and bold, moving out in ever-increasing circles like ripples on a pond.

They pray first that he might bring justice and deliverance to the poor and afflicted. This is always the test of greatness in a ruler – how does he deal with orphans, widows, refugees, the poor? They pray next that the king might give life to the land. They liken him to refreshing rain falling on a mown field, and showers that water the earth. They see righteousness flourishing under his reign and prosperity abounding like crops that grow fertile and life-giving for all.

Third, they pray that his power may go out to the ends of the earth.

They see the king larger than life itself, ruling from sea to sea, his enemies licking the dust, other kings bowing down before him, people of all nations serving him, and all nations calling him blessed. They pray that God's *shalom* blessing may be seen in every area of his life. Blessing for him will mean blessing for all the people.

This is great praying, but, sad to say, no king in Israel's history ever matched this ideal. Shadow and stain marked every ruler, even the greatly loved King David and his wise son King Solomon. But even after the monarchy disappeared, Psalm 72 continued to be read and heard as a proclamation of God's reign and rule in the world. It was in the person of Jesus that the vision of the king portrayed in this psalm was ultimately fulfilled.

## To reflect on
*The power of love displayed on the cross is ultimately the greatest power in the world.*

# MONDAY 6 JANUARY
## Joseph in Trouble

Genesis 39:6–23

'Now Joseph was well-built and handsome, and after a while
his master's wife took notice of Joseph and said,
"Come to bed with me!" ' (vv. 6b,7, NIV).

It was not long before Potiphar's wife took notice of the handsome youth who had become her husband's right-hand man. She minced no words in her adulterous beckoning of Joseph, 'but he refused'. He knew that a sin against her would be, first of all, a sin against his master who had entrusted Joseph with so much. Second, it would be a sin against God. He sounds like David who acknowledges that his adultery with Bathsheba has been, above all, a sin against God. 'Against you, you only, have I sinned and done what is evil in your sight' (Ps 51:4).

She kept on enticing and he kept on refusing, playing safe, guarding against even being with her. Then one day she caught him alone in the house as he attended to his duties. She grabbed his cloak but he struggled free and ran. Enraged and humiliated, she declared to the other workers and then to her husband, 'That Hebrew slave ... came ... to make sport of me.' It was a racial slur and it was a lie, but Joseph was, after all, still only a slave and he had no right of appeal.

Potiphar may have been reluctant to deprive himself of a dependable steward, but he could not ignore his wife's accusation.

Joseph was dismissed on the spot and sent to prison. Not to a common prison, however, but to 'the house of the captain of the guard' (40:3), the place where the king's prisoners were held. The song of God's blessing played its refrain over Joseph, even in prison. 'The LORD was with him' (39:21,23).

In spite of the injustice of his imprisonment, in spite of being the victim yet again of someone else's malice, Joseph did his best to be helpful and to turn a bad situation into good. From being in charge of Potiphar's household, in no time at all Joseph was in charge of Pharaoh's prison.

## To reflect on
*Joseph shows the best move to make against temptation: 'He refused (v. 8) ... he removed (v. 10) ... he ran (v. 12).*

# TUESDAY 7 JANUARY
## Joseph in Prison

Genesis 40:1–23

'Joseph said to them, "Do not interpretations belong to God?
Tell me your dreams" ' (v. 8, NIV).

While Joseph assisted the prison governor with the day-to-day care of the inmates, two men from the royal household were imprisoned. The baker was in charge of preparing Pharaoh's food; the cup-bearer was responsible for tasting and serving his food and wine. If the Pharaoh became unwell, these two men could be held responsible for attempting to poison him.

One morning they both awoke from vivid and puzzling dreams. They were worried, for they knew that 'each dream had a meaning of its own', but in prison they were not free to consult an interpreter. As they spoke to Joseph, he offered to hear their dreams, making it quite clear that God himself was the master dream interpreter.

The cupbearer's dream was of a fruitful vine with three branches budding, blossoming and ripening with grapes, which the cupbearer squeezed into Pharaoh's cup. Joseph's interpretation was reassuring. Within three days the cupbearer would be back at court, serving Pharaoh. Joseph requested no payment for his interpretation, other than a good word spoken on his behalf. 'I was forcibly carried off' ('stolen', NRSV), he explained. 'I have done nothing to deserve being put in a dungeon' (in Hebrew, the same word as 'cistern' in 37:24).

Buoyed up by his colleague's reassuring news, the baker told his dream, which had similarities but a very different interpretation. He dreamed that he was carrying three baskets of bread on his head. Birds came and ate from the top basket, which contained food for Pharaoh. Joseph explained the dream, saying that in three days the baker would be hanged and his body would become food for the birds.

So it came to pass. At a birthday celebration for Pharaoh, these two men were summoned. One had his head lifted up, the other lifted off. In all the turmoil, the cupbearer forgot to mention Joseph's name to Pharaoh. Days in prison rolled into weeks and months, and Joseph was ignored, neglected, overlooked, abandoned, forgotten.

## To reflect on
*Do you ever feel like that? What is God doing when he makes his people wait like this?*

# WEDNESDAY 8 JANUARY
## Joseph Interpreting

Genesis 41:1–16, 28–36

' "I cannot do it," Joseph replied to Pharaoh, "but God will give Pharaoh the answer he desires" ' (v. 16, NIV).

Two long years later, Pharaoh himself had a dream. Two dreams in fact, but one was merely a repeat of the other. Seven sleek (literally 'fat-fleshed') cows were devoured by seven emaciated ('lean-fleshed') cows. Seven heads of grain, 'full and good', were swallowed up by seven other heads, 'thin and scorched by the east wind'. These God-given dreams defied interpretation by Pharaoh's usual advisers, and proved to be Joseph's ticket out of prison. The cupbearer suddenly thought of the young Hebrew who had accurately explained the dreams of the baker and himself while they were in prison.

Pharaoh lost no time in sending for Joseph who was transformed, by means of a shave and a new set of clothing, from prisoner to dream interpreter. He made it quite clear, however, that, while he had no special powers of interpretation, God would give Pharaoh a favourable answer. He sounds like Daniel who, when summoned before King Nebuchadnezzer for a similar task, declared that 'there is a God in heaven who reveals mysteries' (*Dan 2:28*).

Pharaoh recounted his dream and Joseph spoke with confidence. 'God has revealed to Pharaoh what he is about to do.' Seven years of plentiful harvests would be followed by seven years of extreme famine. Joseph made it clear that this was not a judgment for wrong-doing, but rather an act of God that had been firmly decided and revealed in advance so that the kingdom of Egypt could take the necessary steps to prepare for the years of famine.

Without pausing for breath, it seems, Joseph moved from interpreter to strategist, translating God's plan into practical action. 'A wise man . . . in charge . . . collect food . . . store up.' The interpretation was clear, the plan concise, the only question was 'Who?' Pharaoh asked his advisers, 'Can we find anyone like this man, one in whom is the spirit of God?' Then, without hesitating, he pointed to Joseph. 'You . . . you shall be in charge.'

### To reflect on
*It was not Joseph's knowledge of dreams that helped him interpret the meaning. It was his knowledge of God.*

9

# THURSDAY 9 JANUARY
## Joseph in Charge

Genesis 41:37–57

'So Pharaoh said to Joseph, "I hereby put you in charge of the whole land of Egypt" ' (v. 41, NIV).

What a celebration day! In the morning Joseph was a prisoner; by evening he was prime minister, second only to Pharaoh. His responsibilities moved dramatically from Potiphar's house, to the prison house, to Pharaoh's house. The young dreamer who was thrown into a dried-out cistern in Canaan was now put in charge of the whole land of Egypt.

Pharaoh wasted no time in elevating Joseph to royal status. He was given the king's signet ring with which to sign documents. He was dressed in linen robes and given a gold chain of office. He was led in a proclamation procession in a chariot behind Pharaoh's. With an Egyptian name and wife, his makeover was complete. By royal decree Joseph had executive authority throughout the land. His responsibilities took him far and wide. In every city of Egypt he collected grain from the fields and stored it, thus ensuring fair distribution and access to food for the whole population. The grain that he gathered was as vast as the sand of the sea.

The birth of his two sons during the prosperous years helped to establish Joseph's identity as an Egyptian citizen. Although his father-in-law was a priest of the sun god Ra, Joseph gave his children Hebrew names. He called one Manasseh ('made to forget'), for, he said, 'God has made me forget all my trouble and all my father's household.' He would never forget his family, of course, but by an act of will he left the past behind and lived in the present. The name of his second son, Ephraim ('fruitful'), reflected the joy of his birth, saying, 'God has made me fruitful.'

The famine that Joseph had predicted began right on cue, covering Egypt and engulfing the neighbouring countries. News spread and people came to buy grain. Even as Joseph in Egypt resolved to forget his father, his father was thinking of sending his brothers to Egypt. The next twist in God's plan was about to unfold.

## To reflect on
*In what way is the movement of Joseph's life a journey from death to life?*

# FRIDAY 10 JANUARY
## Joseph in Front

---

Genesis 42:1–25, 35–38

---

'Now Joseph was the governor of all the land, the one who sold grain to all its people. So when Joseph's brothers arrived, they bowed down to him with their faces to the ground' (v. 6, NIV).

Back in Canaan, starvation tightened its grip around Joseph's family. Hearing that there was food in Egypt, Jacob sent his sons, but not Benjamin, to buy grain. Of all the food depots they could have come to, by God-chance they happened to arrive at the depot where Joseph was in charge. In submission 'they bowed down to him with their faces to the ground'. Joseph had not forgotten them. As they bowed he remembered dreams of their sheaves of grain bowing down to his. They had aged, but had they changed? Joseph resolved to find out.

Speaking harshly and accusing them of being spies, Joseph put them on the spot and, at the same time, found out what he wanted to know, namely that his father was still alive, as was his younger brother Benjamin. Accusing them of coming to check out the land for military purposes, Joseph put them all in custody for three days. Did that taste like sweet revenge? The brothers insisted on their innocence but Joseph pressed the test by demanding that one brother stay as a hostage while the others went home to fetch Benjamin.

Deeply uneasy at this unexpected turn of events, the brothers spoke among themselves, not realising that Joseph could understand them. They interpreted their present predicament as punishment for what they had done to their brother Joseph, more than twenty years earlier. That guilt was still raw and fresh. Now the tables were turned, even more than they could realise. They had no choice but to leave a brother in custody (as in a cistern) in Egypt while they went home to Canaan with a sorrowful story for their father.

As he listened to them speaking, Joseph turned away and wept. Then he gave orders for Simeon to be detained, while the others were dismissed with their bags full of grain and provisions for the journey. Each brother's money was hidden in his sack. In desperation, they returned to their father in Canaan, not realising that they were in the hands of God's merciful provision and amazing grace.

# SATURDAY 11 JANUARY
## Joseph's Brothers in a Tight Place

Genesis 43:1–14, 26–34

'May God Almighty grant you mercy before the man so that he
will let your other brother and Benjamin come back with you.
As for me, if I am bereaved, I am bereaved' (v. 14, NIV).

In Canaan there was no respite from the famine. With their supplies of grain from Egypt depleted, Jacob once more told his sons to 'go back and buy us a little more food'. But Judah, now spokesman for the brothers, explained that it was useless to go without Benjamin.

For a moment the spotlight falls on Jacob who reveals himself to be a resilient old man. He knows that he is in a no-win situation. Without grain from Egypt they will all die. If the price of going back is Benjamin's life, then so be it. And what about Simeon, still detained in Egypt? This old man has lost one son to wild animals (or so he thinks), another son to an Egyptian prison, and now he has to let his youngest son go. But even as he faces bereavement, he speaks of mercy. 'May God Almighty grant you mercy.' The blood of Abraham runs strongly in the veins of this old man.

There was no choice but to let Benjamin go, his safe return assured by Judah. Jacob told them to take balm, honey, spices, myrrh and nuts, luxury items that would be a rare and welcome gift in Egypt. He ordered them also to take double the amount of silver so they could pay for the first load of grain.

Back in Egypt they were invited to Joseph's house. Frightened at being singled out from all the other famine victims who were buying food, they suspected a trap, or at least punishment for not paying for their first load of grain. But they were mystified when the steward in charge, an Egyptian using Hebrew God-language, assured them that he had received the money. With Simeon safely returned to them, they prepared to meet Joseph.

For the second time they bowed low before the great man. He asked after their father, then spoke a blessing to Benjamin, before he suddenly withdrew. Astonished to be seated according to their birth order, and with Benjamin's plate piled five times higher than anyone else's, the brothers ate, wondering, 'Whatever is going on here?'

# SUNDAY 12 JANUARY
## When Eyes Are Opened

Psalm 73

'My flesh and my heart may fail, but God is the strength of
my heart and my portion forever' (v. 26, NIV).

Psalm 73 opens the third book of the psalms with words of godly wisdom concerning the destiny of the righteous and the wicked. The author, Asaph, the leader of one of David's Levitical choirs, voices a most perplexing problem: Why do the wicked prosper while the godly suffer? It is a question that belongs just as agonisingly to our day as it did to the psalmist's. Why do unruly neighbours, cheats, loan sharks, criminals and terrorists seem to get away with evil, while God's faithful people so often suffer? This psalm is an ancient composition, but it has a contemporary message.

The psalm is Asaph's testimony. He confesses that he was on a slippery path. Troubled and struggling to make sense of life, he became aware of the sleek prosperity of the wicked. They seemed problem-free, sickness-free and carefree. Their arrogant words oozed with self-confidence as they literally got away with murder. The slippery slope for Asaph was that his observations led him to envy. On the very brink of tossing in his faith, he went into God's sanctuary and there, like the prophet Isaiah (*Isa 6:1*), his eyes were opened.

*He saw the wicked in a new way.* He had envied their prosperity and invincibility, but he now saw how fragile those things were. It was not he but they who were on a slippery slope (*v. 18*). In a sudden moment they would lose everything and have nothing left but a dream.

*He saw himself in a new way.* His envy had turned his heart sour and bitter, but meeting with God in the sanctuary gave him God's perspective and reminded him that nothing on earth can compare with the riches of a heart relationship with God.

*He saw the presence of God in a new way.* In that moment of revelation, he knew that, in spite of all the shakings of life, God's constant, loving presence could be relied upon, both in this life and on into eternity.

## To reflect on
*Jesus promised us his presence, not prosperity (Matt 28:20).*

# MONDAY 13 JANUARY
## Joseph in Intrigue

Genesis 44:1–18, 30–34

' "What can we say to my lord?" Judah replied. "What can we say?
How can we prove our innocence? God has uncovered your servants'
guilt. We are now my lord's slaves – we ourselves and the one who
was found to have the cup" ' (v. 16, NIV).

The brothers left for home the next morning with grain in their sacks, and brother Simeon safely restored to them. They must have felt as carefree as the children of Israel, generations later, when they left Egypt for the promised land. But they were stopped in their tracks by Joseph's steward and accused of stealing his master's silver cup, the symbol of Joseph's authority. The brothers were justifiably indignant at such a suggestion. 'Now look here,' they said. 'We are honest men. We paid for our grain and for what we owed from the last time. Why should we steal silver from your master? That's ridiculous!'

In a moment, however, their indignation turned to terror when the cup was found in Benjamin's sack. Knowing full well what this meant, they tore their clothes in grief, and in anguish returned to the city. Once more in Joseph's house, they threw themselves on the ground before him.

From this deep pit of their own making, Judah stepped forward. His explanation to Joseph and his pleading on behalf of his brothers is one of the redemptive themes of this story. As a younger man, Judah had showed scant regard for his brother or his father. He had convinced the others to sell Joseph as a slave (37:27). He had joined his brothers in lying to their father about Joseph's fate (37:32). Then there was the sordid chapter in his own life concerning his daughter-in-law Tamar.

The Judah who stepped forward now, putting his life on the line, was a changed man. He told Joseph how his father Jacob had nearly died over the death of his son Joseph. He declared that if Benjamin did not return, Jacob would die from grief. Crying out, 'I fear to see the suffering that would come upon my father' (v. 34, NRSV), Judah begged to be allowed to stay in place of Benjamin.

### To reflect on
*In Judah's offer to substitute his life for Benjamin's, do you see a picture of what his descendant, Jesus, would do for all the world?*

# TUESDAY 14 JANUARY
## Joseph in Tears

Genesis 45:1–15

'It was not you who sent me here, but God' (v. 8, NIV).

As Joseph listened to Judah offering to be his slave in place of Benjamin, did he recall this same brother, years earlier, encouraging the others to sell Joseph into slavery? Was the picture of his aged father bowed in grief too much for him? All the tangled threads of Joseph's story came together in these moments as, overcome with emotion, he dismissed his attendants and revealed his identity to his brothers. 'I am Joseph!' he cried. 'Come close to me.'

Was this their fondest dream or their worst nightmare coming true before their very eyes? Trembling at what might yet happen, the brothers gathered around Joseph. Could it possibly be true that this was the kid brother they had despised and disposed of more than twenty years earlier?

'You sold me,' said Joseph, 'but God sent me.' Three times he declared that it was not they, but God who sent him ahead of them. His purpose was 'to preserve . . . a remnant on earth and to save your lives by a great deliverance' (v. 7). It was obvious from the famine victims coming to Egypt from many neighbouring countries that this great deliverance applied not only to Joseph's family. Through Joseph, God had made survival possible for countless people during the long period of famine. The murderous intent of Joseph's brothers, when they sold him at Dothan, had been incorporated into God's greater purpose of salvation and deliverance. 'You sold . . . but God sent.'

Those words rang in their ears as the brothers listened to Joseph's instructions. 'Hurry back . . . I will provide for you . . . tell my father . . . bring my father down here quickly.' Joseph threw his arms around Benjamin, then embraced and wept over each of his brothers in turn. His tears of forgiveness mingled with their tears of confession and relief.

## To reflect on
*In the first scene of Joseph's story his brothers 'hated him and could not speak a kind word to him' (37:4). The apparently insignificant detail, now reported, that 'his brothers talked with him', may be the most compelling proof of their transformation.*

# WEDNESDAY 15 JANUARY
## Joseph in Welcome

Genesis 45:16–28; 46:1–7, 28–30

'Joseph had his chariot made ready and went to Goshen to meet his father Israel. As soon as Joseph appeared before him, he threw his arms around his father and wept for a long time' (v. 29, NIV).

Joseph instructed his brothers to hurry back to Canaan with the message, 'God has made me lord of all Egypt', and with the invitation for his father's whole household – children, grandchildren, flocks and herds – to come and settle in Egypt. Pharaoh himself endorsed Joseph's words by promising to give Joseph's father and brothers the best of the land. With carts for the homeward and return journeys, provisions loaded onto donkeys, and lavish gifts for all, they set off, this time with good news for their father. Joseph's final word to them as they left was, 'Don't quarrel on the way!' He was realistic enough to know that the explanation they would have to give their father would be a test for them all.

Jacob's response, on hearing that Joseph was alive and ruler of Egypt, was, understandably, one of shock and disbelief. But with the evidence of carts, provisions and expensive gifts right before his eyes, he was persuaded. This old man, who had endured so much grief, suddenly found a new reason for living: 'I will go and see him before I die.'

Jacob and his whole household travelled south, through areas that were reminiscent of God's dealings with Abraham and Isaac. Years earlier, God had forbidden Jacob's father Isaac to go to Egypt in search of grain (26:2), but that command was not applicable now. Jacob was to be the one to take the family into 'a country not their own' (15:13), where they would become a great nation bearing his God–given name, Israel. Whatever the perils that lay ahead, Jacob knew that the God of his fathers was with him, that he would die in Egypt in the presence of Joseph, and that God would take care of the family, bringing them back eventually to the land of his promise.

Reassured by God's voice 'in a vision of the night', Jacob and his company continued their journey to Goshen, a distinct and separate part of the land of Egypt that was to become their home. There they were met by Pharaoh's warm-hearted welcome, and Joseph's emotional embrace.

# THURSDAY 16 JANUARY
## Joseph in Blessing

---
### Genesis 47:7–12, 27–48:16
---

'May the God before whom my fathers Abraham and Isaac walked,
the God who has been my shepherd all my life to this day . . .
may he bless these boys' (vv. 15,16, NIV).

Reunion with his favourite but long-lost son was the crowning moment of Jacob's life. As they embraced, past sorrows were forgotten. The bitter hatred of Joseph's brothers had been rewarded with kindness and generosity. No wonder the tears flowed!

As Joseph presented his father to Pharaoh, Jacob did not bend low before him, as would have been customary, but blessed him. Joseph settled his family and provided for them as he had promised in an area referred to as 'the district of Rameses'. This royal grant of land was a great honour, an indication of the high esteem in which Joseph was held.

The time came when even Egypt, with its perennial water supply from the Nile, felt the devastating effects of the famine. The people of the land progressively used up all their money, then sold their livestock, their land and eventually themselves in exchange for grain. The Egyptian people were thus reduced to slavery, with the exception of the priests who were provided for from the royal purse, and Joseph's family who settled and greatly multiplied in the land of Goshen.

Jacob lived for seventeen years in this new land, and at the age of 147 knew that he would soon die. He made Joseph promise that he would not be buried in Egypt, but returned to Canaan, the land of promise, and buried in the family tomb in the cave of Machpelah. Joseph's wealth and Egypt's practice of embalming would make such a journey possible. Joseph promised on solemn oath that he would carry out his father's wishes. Unable now to bow on the ground in worship to God, the old man 'worshipped as he leaned on the top of his staff'.

Before he died he blessed Joseph's sons, then each of his sons in turn. Jacob spoke of 'the God who has been my shepherd all my life to this day'. This old man, whose early life had been marred by deceit and scheming, and who had carried a heavy burden of grief from his sons, at the end could speak only blessing and thanksgiving.

# FRIDAY 17 JANUARY
## Joseph in Reassurance

Genesis 50:1–26

'Joseph said to them, "Don't be afraid. Am I in the place of God?
You intended to harm me, but God intended it for good" '
(vv. 19,20, NIV).

With their father dead, mourned, and buried back in Canaan, a new panic arose for Jacob's sons. Joseph had promised his father that he would forgive his brothers and do them no harm. But now that Jacob was dead, would Joseph be true to his word? The brothers sent a message to Joseph, testing the waters, as it were, concealing their anxiety in the fabricated report of a conversation with their father who, they said, encouraged them to ask Joseph to forgive the wrongs they had committed against him.

Hearing the message, Joseph wept. These tears were different from the ones he had shed earlier when he revealed his identity. These tears may have been sadness at the thought of his brothers falsely implicating their father in their story. Or they may have been sorrow at his own failure to reassure them adequately that he had indeed forgiven them. Once more the brothers came and threw themselves down before him. This time it was not before an unknown and powerful Egyptian vizier that they prostrated themselves, but Joseph, their brother, the one they had so murderously despised and on whose mercy they were now so dependent.

Reassuring them, Joseph showed how much he had grown in stature. Now wise, mellowed by the years and by God, he said, 'Don't be afraid. Am I in the place of God? You intended to harm me, but God intended it for good.' Joseph had every right to be bitter towards his brothers, but he chose otherwise. He saw his brothers' dark actions as eclipsed by the merciful and gracious intention of God.

This declaration of faith is the key to Joseph's life. It is like a thread, at times invisible, that has woven its way through his story of rejection, slavery, false accusation, neglect and famine. A greater force than his brothers' jealous hatred has moulded and shaped him. Through dreams and the death of dreams, God has brought him to a place of dream–fulfilment.

## To reflect on
*We live the life of faith forward, but understand it as we look back.*

# SATURDAY 18 JANUARY
## Joseph in Review

Genesis 50:19–26

'You intended to harm me, but God intended it for good
to accomplish what is now being done, the saving of many lives'
(v. 20, NIV).

There are two levels in this story of Joseph and his family. On one level, things happened. A young man was spoilt by his father and despised by his brothers. He had dreams of greatness and was silly enough to tell his family about them. His brothers took their chance one day to silence his dreams for good. They sold him as a slave and he was taken to Egypt where he was wrongfully accused and sent to prison. From there, thanks to his reputation as a dream-interpreter, he was released and put in charge of the land during long years of famine.

So what? Things happen. We could even say, 'He just happened to be spoilt; he just happened to be taken to Egypt; he just happened to be in the right place at the right time or, when it came to Potiphar's wife, in the wrong place at the wrong time.'

But in reading Joseph's story, especially when we read it backwards, as it were, from his great declaration at 50:20, we realise that there is nothing that 'just happened to happen' about him at all. There are no wasted actions, no wasted emotions in this story. Hatred, favouritism, jealousy, distress, grief – they are all vital ingredients that God used to make Joseph the agent, not only of his family's survival, but of the survival of whole nations.

Could it be that our lives are similarly planned? Could it be that there is nothing that 'just happens to happen' to us either, but that everything that happens – graceful and gruesome, beautiful and bad, ordinary and awesome – has God's hand upon it? How would you live if you knew, really knew, that? What difference would it make to you?

Joseph's story invites us to offer to God all that happens to us, both the good and bad done to us and the good and bad that we ourselves have done. This is not a denial of responsibility, but an expression of faith that God can use even the ordinary stuff of our lives to work out his redemptive purposes.

# SUNDAY 19 JANUARY
## Nowhere Else to Turn

### Psalm 74

'But you, O God, are my king from of old;
you bring salvation upon the earth' (v. 12, NIV).

'Why? . . . Why? . . . Why?' This is not a three-year-old asking endless questions of a weary parent, but the psalmist imploring God for answers. He stands in a place of desolation. The temple in Jerusalem has been reduced to rubble, the promised land devastated, the nation of Israel wiped out. In graphic language the psalmist describes the desecration. Hacking, smashing, burning, the enemies of God have destroyed everything in the sanctuary, mocking God all the while. Praise and prayer have been replaced by the profane roaring of pagan soldiers bent on destruction. Why has God let this happen? Why has he not intervened? Why has he turned against his own dwelling place and allowed it to be ruined?

Even worse than the physical devastation is the loss of God's presence and favour. The psalmist speaks of 'the sheep of your pasture' (*v. 1*), 'the people you purchased of old, the tribe of your inheritance' (*v. 2*), as if to remind God of his covenant to care for and protect his people. Israel is like a dove that has been handed over to wild beasts (*v. 19*). The question is, 'Why are you so angry with us?' The plea is, 'Remember' (*vv. 2, 18, 22*).

That word 'remember' becomes the psalmist's own solution as he reviews the great acts of God throughout history and in his own life. The cosmic power of God has been seen in his defeat of enemies. His creative power is seen in the ordered patterns of day and night, sun and moon, summer and winter. The anguished questions remain unanswered but, having voiced his lament, the psalmist turns, not away from God, but towards him in an act of faith.

This is a psalm for those times when our outer world lies in ruins and God seems to have silently taken his leave. There may be no answers to our 'Why' questions, but there is always a call to remember, a Salvation-Bringer to address, and a place of refuge to seek. When all is said and done, there is nowhere else to turn.

# GALATIANS – BOOK OF FREEDOM

## Introduction

Paul's letter to the Galatians has been called 'the Magna Carta of Christian liberty'. In it Paul declares the reality of freedom in Christ – freedom from the law and freedom from the power of sin.

Paul's first missionary journey brought many Gentiles (non-Jews) to faith in Christ. A group of Judaisers, an extremist Jewish faction, followed Paul's trail around the young churches of Galatia and taught the new Gentile Christians that faith in Christ was not enough. They insisted that believers also had to submit to Jewish laws and traditions in order to be accepted by God.

Hearing about this 'Jesus–plus–Moses' gospel, Paul wrote his letter to the Galatian Christians to refute the teachings of the Judaisers and to call believers back to the pure gospel. 'You have been set free,' he said. 'Don't let anyone drive you back into slavery. Salvation is by God's grace through faith in Jesus Christ, and nothing else! Faith in Christ means true freedom.'

Our study of this power–packed letter will raise some deep questions for believers today. What makes a person a Christian – faith in Christ alone, or faith plus adherence to certain principles and practices? At the heart of Paul's letter, the question is: Is the gospel you live by a gospel that sets you free?

> *Set free to worship, I'm set free to praise him,*
> *I'm set free to rejoice before the throne.*
> *So I'll laugh, I'll shout, I'll dance, I'll sing,*
> *Hallelujah, Amen, let the praises ring,*
> *Set free to rejoice for evermore.*
>
> *Thank you, thank you, Lord, for setting me free.*
> *Once I was lost, now I am found,*
> *And my soul is heaven-bound.*
> *Thank you, thank you, Lord, for setting me free.*
> (Composer unknown)

# MONDAY 20 JANUARY
## Under a Banner of Freedom

### Galatians 1:1–5

'Paul, an apostle – sent not from men nor by man, but by Jesus Christ and God the Father, who raised him from the dead' (v. 1, NIV).

Paul's letter to the believers in the Galatian churches is a declaration of freedom. He writes to tell them that, as Christians, they have been set free. This is the banner under which he himself lives.

Paul and Barnabas had just completed their first missionary journey (see *Acts 13:2–14:28*). They had visited Iconium, Lystra and Derbe, cities in the Roman province of Galatia (modern–day Turkey). On returning to Antioch, Paul was accused by some Jewish Christians of watering down Christianity in order to make it more appealing to Gentiles. These Jewish Christians disagreed with Paul's statements that Gentiles did not have to follow many of the religious laws that the Jews had obeyed for centuries – laws such as circumcision, synagogue attendance, the offering of sacrifices, observance of Mosaic rituals and dietary requirements. In this new 'after Christ' era, these zealous teachers were insisting that believers still live in the 'before Christ' tradition.

According to Paul's opponents, Gentiles needed first of all to become card–carrying Jews in order to become Christians. This letter to believers in the churches of Galatia is Paul's response to this distorted theology. He explains that following the Old Testament laws or Jewish rules will not bring salvation. He declares, forcefully and repeatedly, that a person is saved by grace through faith in Jesus Christ. Nothing more, nothing less. He wrote this letter about AD 49, just prior to the meeting of the Jerusalem council, which dealt with the law versus grace controversy (see *Acts 15*).

Paul states his credentials at the very beginning, describing himself, as he does in all his letters, as an apostle (literally 'sent one'). As an ambassador or personal agent of Jesus Christ, he has been sent on a mission with the full authority of the one he represents. Paul is going to have some stern things to say to the believers in the Galatian churches, but at the very beginning of his letter he greets them with 'grace and peace'.

### To reflect on
*Paul's mission was not just his idea – it was God's initiative. Can the same be said about your mission?*

# TUESDAY 21 JANUARY
## The 'Jesus Plus' Gospel

Galatians 1:6–9

*'As we have already said, so now I say again: If anybody is preaching to you a gospel other than what you accepted, let him be eternally condemned!' (v. 9, NIV).*

If Paul's 'grace and peace' greeting makes his readers in the Galatian churches think that this is going to be a gentle, friendly letter, then they are mistaken. Paul comes straight to the point. He is shocked to hear that 'so quickly' – that is, so soon after their conversion – they are deserting to 'a different gospel'. We can almost hear Paul speaking, 'Let me say it as simply as I can. There is no other good news!'

What is it that has him so steamed up? The Galatian Christians, many of whom would have been converted during Paul's first missionary journey, were mainly Greeks who would be unfamiliar with Jewish laws and customs. Some very zealous Jewish Christians, called Judaisers, travelled to the cities where Paul had been to instruct these new Gentile converts in the faith. They preached a 'Jesus Plus' gospel. They taught that, in order to be a true follower, one first of all had to become a Jew. They believed that the Old Testament practices of circumcision and dietary restrictions were required of all believers. The Judaisers may have had a sincere desire to honour their Jewish heritage and help the new converts to integrate it into their faith, or they may have had an underhand motive of questioning Paul's teaching and authority.

Paul does not defend himself, but he leaps to defend the gospel, just as a mother bear would attack anyone who threatens her precious cub. There is no other gospel, Paul declares – no such thing as 'Jesus plus circumcision' or 'Jesus plus dietary rules'. Such teaching is simply a perversion of the gospel. Using the strongest possible language, he condemns anyone – even an angel from heaven – who would preach such a message.

Apply this 'Jesus Plus' gospel to our day and it's easy to identify the things that tempt us to pervert the gospel – Jesus plus good works, Jesus plus duty, Jesus plus self-sacrifice, and so on. Can we, like Paul, truly say:

*He is all I need, he is all I need,*
*Jesus is all I need.*

# WEDNESDAY 22 JANUARY
## A Great Reversal

Galatians 1:10–24

'I did not receive [the gospel] from any man, nor was I taught it; rather, I received it by revelation from Jesus Christ' (v. 12, NIV).

Paul offers no apology for his strong language. This matter of faith is a life–and–death issue. His words are harsh, bold and written in red to warn of danger. Why should the Galatian converts listen to him? Paul's tone changes as he presents his credentials.

He says that the gospel he preached was revealed directly to him by Jesus Christ (v. 12). He had been an exemplary Jew (vv. 13,14), one of the most religious Jews of his day, scrupulously keeping the law and relentlessly persecuting Christians. Before his conversion, he had been even more zealous for the law than the Judaisers were. When it came to religious knowledge and practice, he surpassed everyone else. He was extremely zealous and sincere – but sincerely wrong!

When he met Jesus Christ (vv. 15,16), Paul's life was changed. A complete reversal took place. Where once he pulled down and persecuted believers, now every passion and energy went into building up and encouraging the Church. Other apostles had confirmed him in this ministry (vv. 18,19). Those who had known him in his 'before Jesus' days could only marvel that this zealous persecutor of the Church had become a zealous proclaimer of the gospel of Jesus Christ. Such a transformation could only be explained in God–terms.

These words are Paul's testimony – rugged and real. Notice just who he glorifies as he speaks. He lists his accomplishments but makes it clear that he is now ashamed of those very things, particularly his persecution of Christians. He speaks of his own weakness and declares God's strength. He explains his authority by admitting that he has none of his own. He defends his preaching, not for its theological brilliance but for its source – 'I received it by revelation from Jesus Christ.' His call to become an apostle to the Gentiles was God's initiative. All Paul could do was obey. His biggest claim to fame is that he is a sinner saved by grace.

## To reflect on
*This man, like John the Baptist, is a signpost, pointing away from himself to Jesus Christ. Are you one too?*

# THURSDAY 23 JANUARY
## A Calling to Fulfil

Galatians 2:1–10

'James, Peter and John, those reputed to be pillars, gave me and Barnabas the right hand of fellowship when they recognised the grace given to me. They agreed that we should go to the Gentiles, and they to the Jews' (v. 9, NIV).

Paul has made it clear that the gospel he preaches has been given to him directly from God himself. He now describes the endorsement he received from James, Peter and John, the leaders of the church in Jerusalem. This is Paul holding himself accountable. His discussions clarified for both Paul and Peter that they each have a distinctive task to do. Paul's calling is to preach to the Gentiles; Peter's call is to preach to the Jews. The content is the same for both – that salvation is through faith in Christ – but their congregations are different.

The names that Paul mentions here put a human face on this portion of Scripture. James, Peter and John are familiar figures who walked and talked with Jesus through the Gospels and are now foundation leaders of the young Church. They would have known Paul by reputation at least in his days of frenzied persecution of Christians. Did they share their testimonies as they met together in Jerusalem? Did they marvel at the way in which God led Peter through denial, and Paul through narrow bigotry and hatred, bringing them both to a wide sphere of ministry?

Paul has two travelling companions with him – Barnabas and Titus. Barnabas had been given the name 'Son of Encouragement' by the other apostles. His obedience, reconciling manner, encouraging temperament and dependence on the Holy Spirit earned him a prominent place alongside Paul.

Titus, a Gentile, was possibly one of Paul's early converts (see *Titus 1:4*). Titus is something of a test case. If God has chosen and is using this (uncircumcised) Gentile, then certainly circumcision is not necessary for salvation, nor for joining the people of God. Titus is living proof that salvation is for all people, through the work of Christ, by simply trusting in God's grace.

These names remind us that every believer has a distinctive task to do, a message to deliver, a God-given song to sing.

*To serve the present age,*
*My calling to fulfil,*
*O may it all my powers engage,*
*To do my Master's will!*
**Charles Wesley, SASB 472**

# FRIDAY 24 JANUARY
## Paul versus Peter

Galatians 2:11–14

'When I saw that they were not acting in line with the truth of the gospel, I said to Peter in front of them all, "You are a Jew, yet you live like a Gentile and not like a Jew. How is it, then, that you force Gentiles to follow Jewish customs?" ' (v. 14, NIV).

Paul further demonstrates the authority of the gospel of grace by reporting an issue of conflict between Peter and himself. He tells of an occasion when Peter came to Antioch, a city and major trade centre in Syria. Heavily populated with Greeks, Antioch became the headquarters for the Gentile Church, and Paul's base of operations.

The conflict had to do with food but, for Paul, the issue was far more serious than that. It was the whole matter of salvation. Paul, Peter, some of the zealous Judaisers and some Gentile Christians all gathered to share a meal. Eating together 'with glad and sincere hearts' (*Acts 2:46*) was one of the foundations of fellowship in the young Church, as basic as worship and caring for one another. While Peter had at one time eaten freely with the Gentiles, on this occasion he drew back and ate separately, because he did not want to offend James and his Jewish friends.

Paul reacted! He publicly criticised Peter for violating the gospel. He saw real theological danger in Peter's behaviour. By eating separately, Peter was supporting the Judaisers' view that a believer still had to adhere to certain dietary restrictions, such as what one ate and with whom one ate. In a moment, the smouldering matter became a raging bush fire. The Judaisers accused Paul of watering down the gospel to make it easier for Gentiles to accept, while Paul accused the Judaisers of nullifying the truth of the gospel by adding conditions to it.

Paul declared again that salvation is through faith in Christ alone. It is not through Christ plus adherence to certain Jewish laws and customs. Paul is not reporting this incident in order to make himself look good and Peter look bad, but is using a common, everyday social custom to illustrate that salvation embraces even the ordinary stuff of life. Christ Jesus, he will go on to say, has broken down every barrier that separates people and keeps them apart.

---

*Christ Jesus is our peace – he has broken down every wall (see Eph 2:14–22).*

# SATURDAY 25 JANUARY
## Through Death to Life

Galatians 2:15–21

'I have been crucified with Christ and I no longer live, but Christ lives in me. The life I live in the body, I live by faith in the Son of God, who loved me and gave himself for me' (v. 20, NIV).

Peter and Paul stand as the two giant pillars of the New Testament. They were men of contrast. Practically everything about them was different. Peter's background was that of a fisherman. His world was the wide, open canvas of sea and stars and hard manual labour. Paul came from the world of books and learning, which enhanced his impeccable Jewish heritage.

Peter's conversion story was a long journey of valleys and mountain-tops. His faith began in Jerusalem, was further established in Galilee in close proximity to Jesus, came to a head in his declaration of Jesus as the Messiah, floundered in the Passion week, was revived after the resurrection and came to maturity at Pentecost. By contrast, Paul's conversion story was sudden and dramatic, a total reversal that turned his treasure into trash. The light that shone around him on the road to Damascus both blinded him and, at the same time, opened his eyes to depths of understanding and revelation that he had never before seen.

In spite of all their differences of background and experience, their conversions were essentially identical. They had both turned from death and turned to life. They had both given up trying to be saved by following certain rules, and had found salvation through a simple act of faith in Christ. There was no other way to deal with sin but to nail it to the cross with Jesus. When Jesus died, all that Peter and Paul had prided themselves on had also died, so that they could now say, 'I have been crucified with Christ.' Then when Jesus rose from the dead, they too had been raised to new life, reconciled to God and set free to grow into Christ's likeness.

Our story is different again, but the journey – through death to life – is just the same for us.

## To reflect on
*'Faith is complete trust and complete surrender to Jesus Christ. It is the total acceptance of all that he said, of all that he offered, and of all that he is.'*
*William Barclay*

# SUNDAY 26 JANUARY
## A Cup in the Hand of the Lord

### Psalm 75

'In the hand of the LORD is a cup full of foaming wine mixed with spices; he pours it out, and all the wicked of the earth drink it down to its very dregs' (v. 8, NIV).

Psalm 75 is framed by thanksgiving (*v. 1*) and praise (*vv. 9,10*), but the heart of the psalm is a song of judgment against the wicked. Arrogant worldly powers threaten Israel's security. The moral order of the world seems to have crumbled. The people of God are shaken. Using three powerful word pictures, the psalmist, Asaph, speaks a word of reassurance.

The first picture is of the great pillars of the earth that hold the world steady even in the midst of the shaking (*v. 3*). The psalmist is writing at a time of great upheaval and disorder, days not unlike our own. In Psalm 11 the psalmist, David, had asked, 'When the foundations are being destroyed, what can the righteous do?' Here Asaph gives an answer, 'Keep your trust in the God who holds the world steady.'

The second picture is that of a foaming cup of wine in the hand of God (*v. 8*). The wine has been mixed with spices to make it even more intoxicating. God's people know about the cup of salvation (*Ps 116:13*), the cup of joy (*Ps 23:5*), the cup of thanksgiving (*1 Cor 10:16*), but this cup in the hands of God is a cup of judgment and humiliation. He is ready to pour it down the throats of all the world's boastful, till the last dregs are swallowed.

The third picture is of horns, mentioned four times in this psalm. The horn was a symbol of power, majesty and dignity, which could be raised in honour or defiance. God's promise here is that the horns of the wicked will be cut off, but the horns of the righteous will be lifted up in triumph (*v. 10*).

When our outer world is shaken by the upsurge of evil powers, or when our inner world is shattered by loss and overwhelming sorrow, there is a place of refuge and rest. God, who holds the pillars of our world secure, is still gloriously in charge. 'As for me,' concludes the psalmist, 'I will declare this forever.'

*May his conclusion be your confidence today!*

# MONDAY 27 JANUARY
## Lay Your Burden Down

Galatians 3:1–14

'Are you so foolish? After beginning with the Spirit,
are you now trying to attain your goal by human effort?' (v. 3, NIV).

I recall the story of a man who was trudging along a country road, carrying a heavy pack on his back. A man on a cart pulled by a donkey stopped and offered him a ride. The traveller clambered up onto the cart, but sat with the heavy pack still on his back. After a while, the driver noticed and told the man to put his load down onto the tray of the cart. 'Oh no,' replied the passenger. 'I'm afraid it might be too heavy for your donkey.' Silly man!

The Galatian believers were doing something similar, but Paul uses much stronger language to tell them off. 'You foolish Galatians!' he says or, as *The Message* puts it, 'You crazy Galatians!' They have become fascinated by and fallen under the spell of the arguments of the false teachers who say that Gentiles have to become Jews in order to become Christians.

Some of these Galatian believers may have been in Jerusalem at Pentecost. They may have known those days of prayer and longing and waiting for the promised Holy Spirit to come. When he came, with signs of wind and fire and tongues that could only be explained in God-terms, they received the Holy Spirit, and thus witnessed the birth of the Church.

Paul fires out his questions. Did they receive the Holy Spirit by following the law of Moses? Of course they did not. They were saved by faith in Christ and they will grow into Christian maturity in the same way. Not by human effort, not by following special rules. Toss the heavy burden off your backs, he says, it's just weighing you down.

Paul quotes from Habakkuk 2:4, declaring, 'The righteous will live by his faith.' The load of sin has been removed and believers are now set free to live each day in forgiveness and newness of life. There is only one response to that – Hallelujah!

*Shackled by a heavy burden,*
*'Neath a load of guilt and shame,*
*Then the hand of Jesus touched me,*
*And now I am no longer the same!*
*William and Gloria Gaither*[1]

# TUESDAY 28 JANUARY
## The Covenant of Faith

Galatians 3:15–18

'If the inheritance depends on the law, then it no longer depends on a promise; but God in his grace gave it to Abraham through a promise' (v. 18, NIV).

Paul's words in this portion of his letter to the Galatians reach right back to the book of Genesis and the covenant that God made with Abraham. We think of a covenant as a mutual agreement between two equal parties – 'You do this and I'll do that. Agreed. Let's shake on it.' But the covenant that God made with Abraham was a one-sided promise, initiated by God and offered unreservedly to Abraham. God promised to give Abraham offspring, blessing, a great name, occupancy of the promised land, and the assurance that he would always be the God of Abraham and of his descendants (see *Gen 17:1–8*). This was a covenant that could never be revoked, added to or changed.

Abraham's part in this covenant was not that of an equal partner, but merely that of a recipient. By faith he received what God promised to give and by faith his descendants would continue to receive God's blessings.

Much later than Abraham, in fact over 400 years later, the law of Moses was given. As the people of God met together at Mount Sinai, Moses gave them the Ten Commandments. These commandments were to give the people guidelines for living, but did not take the place of God's earlier covenant with Abraham. Faith was still the key for living a God-life. The law simply provided the guidelines for action.

I borrow Paul's words and say, 'Let me take an example from everyday life' (*v. 15*). My husband is a keen gardener and in the spring he plants out our summer garden. Many of the young plants can be planted and left, but some vegetables, such as runner beans, need support. They grow so quickly that they need poles for the tendrils of the beans to twine around as they grow. In the same way, the laws of Moses are like support poles that give guidelines for action in the life of faith.

## To reflect on
*What or who are the support poles that help you grow in your life of faith? Name them and give thanks to God for them today.*

# WEDNESDAY 29 JANUARY
## The Purpose of the Law

Galatians 3:19–25

'Before this faith came, we were held prisoners by the law, locked up until faith should be revealed' (v. 23, NIV).

Paul asks the obvious question – 'What, then, was the purpose of the law?' (*v. 19*). He has stated that the law of Moses came over 400 years after God's covenant with Abraham. The law did not replace the covenant, so did it have any benefit at all? Indeed it did. On the positive side, the law showed people how to live. Like the bean poles in yesterday's reading, the law gave believers guidelines for living the life of faith.

On the negative side, the law pointed out people's sin and showed that it is impossible to please God simply by obeying his laws. Think of the rich young ruler who came to Jesus, asking questions about eternal life (see *Matt 19:16*). When it came to keeping the laws of Moses, he had a perfect record, but he knew that he still lacked something (*v. 20*). Jesus told him to go and sell his possessions, for it was not his actions that could save him, but the heart attitude that needed to put God, not wealth, in first place.

The law, Paul says, kept us locked up. It was like a prison guard who played malicious games with us, trapping us in our sins and offering us no way out. It beat us up for our past mistakes. It held us in a head-lock and choked us for our wrong attitudes. It rendered us helpless, unable to do anything to save ourselves. God saw our plight and knew we were sin's prisoners, and he provided a way of escape – the death of Jesus Christ. This happened, Paul told the believers in Rome, 'at just the right time, when we were still powerless' (*Rom 5:6*).

So the law did have a purpose. It gave us guidelines for living, but also made us acutely aware that, because of our sins, even the strictest adherence to the law could never make us righteous. Just as slave-tutors in Paul's day took the children in their charge to school, so the law led us to Christ.

### To reflect on
*What need brought you to Christ?*

# THURSDAY 30 JANUARY
## All One in Christ

Galatians 3:26–29

'There is neither Jew nor Greek, slave nor free, male nor female,
for you are all one in Christ Jesus' (v. 28, NIV).

Paul masterfully states and restates his case throughout his letter – acceptance by God and a continued relationship with him cannot be achieved by following certain laws, but comes by faith, and is for people of all kinds. Using another example from everyday life, he describes believers as sons of God. This has nothing to do with masculinity or manliness, for Paul states, in the same breath as it were, in Christ there is 'neither . . . male nor female'.

Paul's emphasis here is on the word 'all', which is the first word of the sentence in Greek. It is this word that the Judaisers would find particularly offensive. They believed that the only way these Galatian 'half-converts' could become 'full-converts' was by following certain Jewish laws. But Paul is saying that all – that is, every believer, both Greek and Jew, slave and free, male and female – are accepted by God simply through faith. In one sentence Paul challenges the long-held prejudice behind the prayer that some Jews prayed every day: 'Blessed be God that he did not make me a Gentile, a slave or a woman.' National, social and gender distinctions that once governed and separated people have now been broken down. These labels are no longer relevant. With the coming of Christ, 'all' have become 'one'.

In Roman society, a youth coming of age would lay aside the robe he had worn throughout his childhood and put on a new toga. This was an outer indication that he had moved from being a child to becoming an adult, with all the rights and responsibilities of adulthood. Paul uses this illustration to explain what happens when a believer is baptised into Christ. 'Your baptism in Christ was not just washing you up for a fresh start. It also involved dressing you in an adult faith wardrobe' (v. 27, *The Message*).

In one broad stroke he concludes: Anyone who is in Christ is the seed of Abraham and an heir to the promised blessing of God.

*Rejoice today, believer, that you are now clothed in the new robe of (Christ's) righteousness.*

# FRIDAY 31 JANUARY
## A Slave or a Son?

Galatians 4:1–7

'So you are no longer a slave, but a son; and since you are a son,
God has made you also an heir' (v. 7, NIV).

Paul has made his point clear. Anyone who is 'in Christ' is a child of God and entitled to receive all that God has promised. He now expands the illustration further to show that the Judaisers are completely wrong in demanding that converts follow the Jewish laws in order to be fully saved.

A child, says Paul, who is destined to inherit an estate is no different from a slave, as long as he is a child, for he cannot inherit the father's estate until he becomes an adult. During this period he is subject to guardians and trustees, but only until the father's set time of inheritance. Paul likens the 'childhood period' to the period of the law and the 'inheritance period' to the time brought about by Jesus Christ. The time of following the law was the time of slavery; the time of faith in Christ is the time of freedom.

'We were in slavery,' says Paul, when we were children learning the 'ABCs' of God's revelation. But 'when the time had fully come' we were made sons. God is like a father who sets the time for a child to receive his inheritance. God sent his Son to live under the law so that he could absorb the curse of the law and redeem those under the law. Once Jesus had done this, the barrier between God and people was broken down and, as a result, all believers have become 'sons of God'. No longer slaves, but now sons, believers are heirs to all that God has promised. This new relationship means that every believer is entitled to use the term 'Abba' to address God. This Aramaic term for 'father' was the intimate word that Jesus used in his relationship with God.

Paul's logic flows on, unstoppable. Since believers have received God's inheritance by faith, they no longer need to live according to the law. Any demand that they do so is simply, blatantly, unarguably wrong!

## To reflect on
*Are you a slave, still under the law, or, by faith, a son and heir of God's promises?*

# SATURDAY 1 FEBRUARY

## Paul the Pastor

Galatians 4:8–20

'My dear children, for whom I am again in the pains of childbirth until Christ is formed in you' (v. 19, NIV).

Paul's love and intense concern for the Galatian believers overflows in this passage of his letter. Elsewhere he called them 'foolish Galatians!' (*3:1*), but here his tone softens and he addresses them as 'brothers' and 'my dear children'. He states the problem and then gives a heartfelt plea.

These Galatian converts were typical pagans who did not know the God of Israel, the true God of the whole world. The gods they did know were not real gods at all, merely 'paper tigers' (*The Message*). The day came when they were wonderfully converted as a result of Paul's preaching, and they came to know the true God in a real way, and to be known by him.

The problem is, however, that this great beginning has faltered. In spite of all they have received from God, they have reverted to their old ways. Their adherence to the rituals and observances of Judaism has simply been a return to paganism. 'How can you do that?' Paul asks, puzzled and disappointed. In Paul's mind, anything that takes the place of total reliance upon Jesus Christ is not real Christianity at all. His fear is that all his efforts on their behalf have been wasted.

This is Paul the pastor speaking, grave and concerned for these people whom he loves so dearly and into whose lives he has invested so much. He reminds them of how warmly they welcomed him when, because of illness, he went to Galatia. They treated him as if he were an angel of God, or even Jesus Christ himself.

Paul is not into calling people to follow him, however. His is no personality cult. In urging them to 'become like me' (*v. 12*), he is begging them to guard against becoming enslaved once again to what they have already been freed from. He longs for them to become fully mature in Christ.

### To reflect on

*Paul's words of love and longing are the words of every pastor, every discipler who invests time and effort into a new Christian. May you be encouraged in that 'birthing' task today.*

# SUNDAY 2 FEBRUARY
## A Song of Zion

Psalm 76

'His tent is in Salem, his dwelling-place in Zion' (v. 2, NIV).

This psalm has traditionally been called a Song of Zion. It is a song of Zion's past and a song for Zion's people. The city of Jerusalem with its great temple was seen to be the earthly dwelling place of God, the indestructible capital of the world. But the city was not indestructible for it was destroyed in 587 BC by the Babylonians and again in AD 70 by the Romans.

The psalm is full of strong war-like imagery – flashing arrows, shields and swords, weapons of war (v. 3). God is the mighty Lion-Warrior of Israel whose 'den' is on Mount Zion. 'The LORD roars from Zion and thunders from Jerusalem,' proclaimed the prophet Amos (*Amos 1:2*). The psalmist declares by the end of the psalm that the whole world is under God's lion-like control. He will break the strength of any who oppose.

The violent imagery should not offend or frighten us. The psalmists and prophets saw with the eye of faith and wrote about a day when the sounds of war would be silenced and weapons of destruction would be hammered into farm equipment (see *Isa 2:4; Micah 4:3*). We live in a fragile world. Jerusalem, symbol of God's eternal, covenant presence, is still war-torn and fought over. But God will have the final word.

*Jerusalem: a name, a secret. For the exiled, a prayer. For all others, a promise. Jerusalem: seventeen times destroyed yet never erased. The symbol of survival. Jerusalem: the city which miraculously transforms man into pilgrim; no one can enter it and go away unchanged.*

Elie Wiesel, *A Beggar in Jerusalem*

Psalm 76 is a call to a pilgrim people, an invitation to live under God's sovereignty, to adopt God's values and God's ways, and to work and wait for God's day of peace.

---

*Glorious things of thee are spoken,*
*Zion, city of our God;*
*He whose word cannot be broken*
*Formed thee for his own abode.*
*On the rock of ages founded,*
*What can shake thy sure repose?*
*With salvation's walls surrounded,*
*Thou mayest smile at all thy foes.*
**John Newton, SASB 157**

# MONDAY 3 FEBRUARY
## Drawing the Lines

Galatians 4:21–31

'Now you, brothers, like Isaac, are children of promise' (v. 28, NIV).

Paul, sounding like a rabbi once again, now brings his teaching to a climax. He uses another graphic illustration, this time from Jewish history, to make his point against the Judaisers and their insistence that the Galatian converts follow the Mosaic laws. He allegorises the Old Testament story of Sarah and her maidservant, Hagar. These women gave birth to Abraham's sons, Isaac and Ishmael (see *Gen 16 and 21*).

The two women correspond to two covenants and two ways of relating to God. Hagar represents the covenant established on Mount Sinai, where the law was given to Moses. Her children are all slaves because they live according to the Mosaic law. Such revolutionary teaching, that those who obey the law are slaves in the line of Ishmael, would sound shocking to the Judaisers.

In contrast, Sarah represents the covenant established in the 'heavenly Jerusalem'. Childless Sarah was described as 'barren' (*Gen 11:30*), but Isaac, child of faith, was born to her. The prophet Isaiah declared that the barren woman should rejoice, for God would give her countless children who, through faith, would be free citizens of that heavenly city (*Isa 54:1*). Those who believe in Christ, says Paul, are already living in this new era of fulfilment of God's promise.

Paul draws the lines clearly. Now you, brothers, he says, are not children of the slave woman, like Ishmael. You are children of promise, like Isaac. Just as Ishmael, the slave child, persecuted the free child, Isaac, so true believers in Christ are being persecuted by the 'Moses plus Christ' Judaisers. The only solution is for the Galatian believers to expel the Judaisers, just as Sarah expelled Hagar and her son.

Paul's illustration of Sarah and Hagar might sound a long way from our day, but it would have great resonance with his audience. Having drawn the lines, his urgent call to all believers is to 'get rid of' (*v. 30*) anything that would stand in freedom's way.

## To reflect on
*Which side of the line do you stand on – in the freedom of faith or in slavery to the law?*

# TUESDAY 4 FEBRUARY
## Here's to Freedom!

Galatians 5:1

'It is for freedom that Christ has set us free' (v. 1, NIV).

Paul's call for freedom is the very essence of his letter to the Galatians and the very heart of the gospel. The purpose of Christ's work was to set Jews free from the curse of the law and to allow Gentiles to enjoy the same liberation by breaking their chains of disobedience and sin. In as many ways as he can, Paul has repeated this message.

The English translation of this verse fails to capture the strong emphasis of the words in Greek. 'Freedom . . . you . . . Christ . . . set free'. In Greek, four words say it all, forcefully and unforgettably. But what exactly is meant by freedom?

For Paul, 'being free' means being in relationship with God. 'Being free' is the result of the death of Jesus Christ who redeemed sinners from the burden of the law. 'Being free' is life in the Spirit of God. Paul said later, 'Through Christ Jesus the law of the Spirit of life set me free from the law of sin and death' (*Rom* 8:2). The freedom that Paul writes of is a divine work of grace, the life of God won for us by Jesus and given to us by the Holy Spirit. This is the theological dimension of freedom.

For Paul, freedom also has a personal dimension. The freedom that God gives is from everything that would shackle or bind us, the freedom to become all that God wants us to be. Freedom also has a social dimension. God sets us free through Jesus Christ and in the Spirit, so that we can love God and others.

I recall as a teenager reading the words of John Newton, who said, 'I am not what I ought to be, I am not yet what I long to be. But by the grace of God I am not what I was, and I am what I am.' Those words set me free to move out of the narrow confines of my own world and to reach out to others.

## To reflect on
*Why not run a 'freedom check' on yourself today?*

# WEDNESDAY 5 FEBRUARY
## In a Nutshell

Galatians 5:2–12

'For in Christ Jesus neither circumcision nor uncircumcision has any value. The only thing that counts is faith expressing itself through love' (v. 6, NIV).

Paul is like a person who, given the task of preparing banners for a protest march, paints hundreds of banners with a single word on each, 'Freedom!' Having waved his banner high, Paul now proceeds to apply the matter of freedom to the pressing issue of circumcision. Will the Galatians follow Paul's 'law-free' gospel, or will they succumb to the teachings of the Judaisers, which combined the gospel of Jesus Christ with the laws of Moses?

The point at issue is not just circumcision itself. 'Neither circumcision nor uncircumcision has any value,' he says. Rather, Paul contends that if, because of the influence of the Judaisers, the Galatians go ahead with circumcision, they will be opening a veritable can of worms. They will be admitting, in the act of submitting to the rite, that they think that Christ is insufficient, that the Spirit is not a good guide for living, that the laws of Moses need to be obeyed for acceptance by God, and that one needs to become a Jew to become a child of God. In other words, if they let themselves be persuaded by the Judaisers on this one point, then 'Christ will be of no value ... at all' (v. 2).

This action will have a number of reactions. Submitting to one aspect of the law of Moses will oblige them to follow the whole law, with the result that they will be separated from Christ and grace, and they will miss what really matters, which is faith. Using one of his favourite images, Paul likens the Galatians' Christian life to a race, but says that someone has obviously cut in on them and hindered their successful run of 'obeying the truth' (v. 7).

In two verses (vv. 5,6), Paul gives a masterful summary of his whole letter. He draws together the threads of faith, the Spirit of God, righteousness, future hope, love and the argument against circumcision. This is the letter of Galatians in a nutshell.

## To reflect on
*Can you identify anyone or anything that cuts in on you and keeps you from obeying the truth?*

# THURSDAY 6 FEBRUARY
## Free to Sin . . . Free to Serve

Galatians 5:13–26

'You, my brothers, were called to be free. But do not use your freedom to indulge the sinful nature; rather, serve one another in love' (v. 13, NIV).

Paul waves his freedom banner high once again. He has explained that the life of faith in Christ Jesus is characterised by freedom from the law and its bondage. Submitting to even one demand of the law, namely circumcision, would mean abandoning Jesus Christ and the grace of God.

The Judaisers insisted that believers needed the law of Moses. If they did not have the law, they would have no clear guidelines for living, and in no time would fall into indulgence and immorality. Paul contends, however, that freedom from the law is not a licence for wickedness. He says that the only way to avoid living according to the flesh ('the sinful nature', NIV) is to live in love, which, after all, is the very essence of the whole law distilled into one command.

To make his point clear, Paul describes the acts of the sinful nature. There are sexual sins – immorality, impurity and debauchery; religious sins – idolatry and witchcraft; social sins – hatred, discord, jealousy, fits of rage, selfish ambition, dissensions, factions and envy; drinking

sins – drunkenness and orgies. Living according to these dictates of the flesh will only lead to excess, addictions and slavery. Freedom to sin is no freedom at all.

Living according to the Spirit, however, will produce fruit in the believer's life – attitudes towards God of love, joy and peace; qualities of patience, kindness and goodness in human relationships; personal principles of faithfulness, gentleness and self-control in one's conduct.

These two lists face each other like opposing football teams at the start of a game. Choose carefully which side you are on, says Paul. Give up the biting and devouring (v. 15), the factions that are destroying you from the inside. Set a new course for yourselves – live by the Spirit. In that way, you will discover what true freedom is all about.

## To reflect on
*Paul's call to crucify the sinful nature (v. 24) and to keep in step with the Spirit (v. 25) is a call to death and life. How is that call worked out each day in your life?*

# FRIDAY 7 FEBRUARY
## Burdens and Backpacks

---
### Galatians 6:1–10
---

'Therefore, as we have opportunity, let us do good to all people, especially to those who belong to the family of believers' (v. 10, NIV).

Paul could never be accused of saying to Peter or James, 'You two deal with the practical side of being a Christian, and leave the theology to me.' In all Paul's writings, and not the least in this letter, his teaching is grounded in everyday application of what it means to live as a Christian individual within a community of believers.

His instructions about bearing burdens, sharing with one's teacher, sowing and reaping, and doing good, may seem unrelated to each other, but they need to be seen against the backdrop of strife and division, the 'biting and devouring' (5:15), of the Galatian churches. Two strong themes emerge – personal responsibility and mutual accountability.

Paul makes what sounds like a contradiction – 'carry each other's burdens' (v. 2), and 'each one should carry his own load' (v. 5). But the picture behind the first is that of an overwhelming weight, while the picture behind the second is that of a backpack. Christians need to help one another in the struggles of life, but each Christian will have to answer to God individually.

In her line drawings in the Good News Bible, Swiss artist Annie Vallotton has illustrated Paul's call by drawing a line of people, each one bearing a load of differing size, and each person holding a supportive hand under the load of the person in front.

The community of faith ('you who are spiritual') must be characterised by graciousness. Restoring a Christian brother or sister must be done gently (literally 'in a spirit of humility'). There is no room for pride or comparison with others. Every action has a reaction, Paul says. You will reap what you sow. Sow gossip and you'll reap heartache. Sow kindness and you'll grow kindness. Finally, he says, take every opportunity to do good or, in other words, to sow a harvest of goodness to all people, regardless of their culture, nationality or gender (see 3:28), and especially to fellow believers.

---

### To reflect on
*Today, as you carry your own 'backpack', look for an opportunity to help someone else carry their heavy load.*

# SATURDAY 8 FEBRUARY
## Boasting and Blessing

Galatians 6:11–18

'May I never boast except in the cross of our Lord Jesus Christ, through which the world has been crucified to me, and I to the world' (v. 14, NIV).

Paul's letter to this point was probably dictated to a scribe, but he now takes the pen himself to bring it to conclusion. The 'large letters' he uses may be for emphasis, or they may be evidence of his poor eyesight. For one last time he states his strong opposition to the teachings of the Judaisers. He has no time for any presentation of the gospel that does not put surrender to Jesus Christ and life in the Spirit as the priority.

Paul identifies four problems with the Judaisers. First, their method is force. They have been trying to force the Galatians to accept circumcision as the outward sign of conversion. They have been telling these new converts, 'To be accepted by God you must do this.'

Second, their motive is fear. The Judaisers were being pressured by the Jerusalem Jews to bring Paul's converts into line with the basic teachings of Judaism. But Paul sees this pressure as simply being a denial of the gospel. The cross of Christ has put an end to the demands of the law.

Third, their consistency is flawed.

The Judaisers themselves do not practise what they preach. While insisting on circumcision as a sign of conversion, they themselves are ignoring other demands of the law.

Fourth, their goal is to flaunt. These scalp hunters want only to return to Jerusalem and boast that Paul's converts are now their converts.

While they glory in the flesh, says Paul, I glory in the cross of Christ. The world and its demands mean nothing to him. Even if being a Christian means persecution, he would still glory. What really matters is not circumcision (being a Jew), nor uncircumcision (being a Gentile), but being part of the new people of God. As he has said before, in God's new creation the old national, social and gender distinctions that once separated people no longer mean anything (3:28).

Paul began his letter with curses for those who preach a different gospel (1:6–9). He concludes with a blessing of peace and mercy to all who live according to God's new creation.

# SUNDAY 9 FEBRUARY
## The God of Unseen Footprints

Psalm 77

'Your path led through the sea, your way through the mighty waters, though your footprints were not seen' (v. 19, NIV).

Psalm 77 is the prayer–psalm of all who lie awake at night, pondering the deep questions. Asaph, the psalmist, is in distress, but his is not the distress of a passing sadness or a sudden tragedy. His whole life has been blanketed by a dark and heavy sorrow that refuses to budge. The strong verbs express his exhaustion, 'I cried out ... I sought the Lord ... I stretched out untiring hands ... my soul refused to be comforted ... I groaned ... my spirit grew faint ... I was too troubled to speak.'

In spite of Asaph's urgent cries for help, however, God has turned silent, thus making a miserable situation even worse. It seems the psalmist has tried all the usual ways of summoning the sense of God's nearness, 'I mused ... I remembered ... my spirit enquired', but what may have once worked well has this time simply failed. If days were once favoured with God's presence, they are no longer. Songs of praise, sung so confidently in the past, are now stilled.

The desperate questions rise up like ghosts in the night. Will the God who did such marvellous things in the past ever do them again? Will his steadfast love continue? Has he changed his mind about being a compassionate God and become, instead, angry and vengeful? Will the psalmist's anguished questions ever stop their dark, taunting midnight dance?

His focus on 'I' in the first half of the psalm turns to 'You' in the second half. He remembers and meditates on what God has done. He recounts the mighty demonstration of God's power in creation and in the deliverance of his people. He knows that God is Creator, Deliverer and Shepherd, but even these strong images are not enough to bring an end to his deep questions and weary waiting. Like us, the psalmist grapples with a God who at times leads his people so clearly and, at other times, leaves no trace of footprints at all.

## To reflect on
*When God seems absent, he may in fact be more present than ever.*

# THE SALVATION PROJECT

## Introduction

Major Seth Le Leu is a New Zealand officer who has served most of his officership outside his home country. As a young officer he went with his family to Zambia, where he and his wife Pamela served as teachers at the Chikankata Secondary School. This was followed by eleven years in Tanzania, where they were the leaders for seven years. Now they both serve at International Headquarters coordinating community development programmes in the developing world. Seth writes:

Those of us who use the Internet regularly will often come to a new web site with anticipation. The name sounds good. It should have all the information we need and we find the sign: 'This site is under construction. Visit us soon.' We click again and move on to somewhere else. So it is with the Salvation Project. It is a site under construction. God has done so much already, but the project is not finished. Its results are not all recorded. When the project is completed we won't need devotional books like this one, for we will be with the Lord himself in a new heaven and a new earth.

In my work as the Salvation Army's coordinator of the community development programme around the world, I thought that it would be helpful, in preparation for Easter, to stand back and look at the whole Plan of Salvation, using the framework of project planning. In this framework we see God's big goal is to restore the world to its rightful state. In the process he deals with Satan's rebellion and establishes his kingdom here on earth in the form of his Church. But it is not all finished. Satan's hand is still seen in so many ways. God's kingdom is still not fully established. This is a site under construction. But don't move on. Stay and have a look. Maybe there are some important things this site can show you.

# MONDAY 10 FEBRUARY
## The Salvation Project

Ephesians 1:3–10

'He thought of everything, provided for everything we could possibly need, letting us in on the plans he took such delight in making . . . a long-range plan in which everything would be brought together and summed up in him, everything in deepest heaven, everything on planet earth' (vv. 9,10, *The Message*).

As the Salvation Army's coordinator for development programmes around the world, I am often asked to assist people in the preparation of their plans for development. We use the project format to assist communities to achieve goals that will improve their quality of life. A project is the application of a finite set of resources to a finite activity over a finite period of time.

We can use the project metaphor to gain a clearer picture of God's eternal plan. God's Salvation Project applies a finite set of resources – the universe and all created beings – to a finite activity – the preparation of a people for himself – over a finite period of time – this span we call chronological time.

In the preparation of projects, one of the tools we use is called the logical framework analysis. This is an excellent tool to help plan activities in a timely and efficient way. In these meditations we will look at God's Salvation Project and use the 'log frame' as our analysis. God's goal is simple: 'To restore everything to himself through Jesus Christ.'

In the plan we will find our place and God's place and we will also find out where we are in the timeframe of the project. Easter has a vital place in the whole Salvation Project, for it was at that critical point in God's project that all the elements of the plan were brought together.

A key tool we use in project planning is to evaluate everything that happens to see if it contributes to the project's goal. Similarly, as we see the Planner's hand guiding and controlling history, we will perceive that, in the randomness of our present circumstances, God is omnipresent and is working out his will in the world. I trust we will discover, with wonder, that his great goal of restoring all things to himself is being worked out in us as well. We are not governed by random fate. We are children of a king, part of his Salvation Project.

# TUESDAY 11 FEBRUARY
## Keeping Your Eye on the Goal

Ephesians 1:11,12

'It's in Christ that we find out who we are and what we are living for'
(v. 11, *The Message*).

In the early morning light during the ploughing season in Africa, the fields are busy with activity. Sometimes two or, if the farmer is wealthy, four oxen are yoked together. The test of the farmer's skill is to demonstrate how well he can plough his land. The oxen soon begin to steam with the effort. The work proceeds fitfully, for oxen are not machines and they need to be encouraged.

The earth is turned over, revealing its dark texture, and the birds are on hand to feast on the worms. I asked a farmer, 'How do you plough such beautifully straight lines?' He replied, 'I fix my eyes on an object at the far end of the field and walk towards it in a straight line. If I look down I lose my way.' Good ploughing requires an eye kept on the goal.

In project work the goal is a particular change or object that has been agreed upon. If you fix your eye on the goal, then it is easy to see which resources and activities you need to have in order to reach that goal. Without a firm goal, many resources and much time can be spent in activities that achieve little

of lasting benefit. Once the goal is fixed, the activities to achieve that goal can be adapted. At the end of the process, the project will be evaluated against that one thing – did the project achieve its goal?

God's Salvation Project is no different. All the activity engaged in at the present time has a place and purpose in the mind of the Project Manager. From our perspective we may not understand what is happening. But the patient hand of the Father is present in his world, guiding it to its ultimate goal. We are all part of that plan and he uses our everyday willingness to achieve his goal.

Let's not get sidetracked by daily distractions, but let us keep our eyes firmly fixed on the goal of God's great plan, which is to restore this world to himself.

# WEDNESDAY 12 FEBRUARY
## To Destroy the Rebellion

John 12:31–33

'Jesus said . . . "At this moment the world is in crisis. Now Satan, the ruler of this world, will be thrown out" ' (v. 31, *The Message*).

In project planning, once the goal has been established, the next thing to do is to establish the objectives. The objectives describe the different parts of the whole project. In the case of the Salvation Project, the goal is for God to restore all things to himself. One of the objectives, then, is to destroy the rebellion that stole creation in the first place.

As I grew up, the *Stars Wars* series of movies captured my imagination. Here I saw the efforts of the war between those who followed the dark side of the force and those who followed the right side. I recall one encounter between the hero, Luke Skywalker, and the villain, who was called the Emperor. The Emperor was tempting Luke to change sides but Luke, in true heroic tradition, resisted the temptation.

This Hollywood story actually mirrors the eternal reality. One of God's great objectives in the Salvation Project is to put down Satan's rebellion, a rebellion in which Satan stole the rule of the world from humankind. Easter is the place where the key victory occurs in this battle. Jesus says these words in today's reading: 'The world is in crisis, but Satan's present rule over the earth will be destroyed.' At that critical moment, on the cross, when Jesus said the words, 'It is finished!', he meant that Satan's stranglehold on this world had been broken.

Events in the world today might tell us otherwise. The world around us seems to be in crisis, but God's great objective is being worked out. Satan's power is broken! Hallelujah! I encourage you to live confidently today in the light of that truth.

## A prayer for today

*Loving God, as we see the crises in our world, let our hearts be at rest. Even though evil still seems to be everywhere, we know, from what Jesus has done, that Satan's evil rule has been broken. We are on the winning side! In your Spirit's power, may we walk through this day as your occupation forces in the world.*

# THURSDAY 13 FEBRUARY
## To Establish a Holy People

1 Peter 2:9

'But you are a chosen people, a royal priesthood, a holy nation, a people belonging to God' (v. 9, NIV).

One of the great objectives in the Salvation Project is God's intention to gather together a people who belong to him. From the time of my namesake, Seth (see *Gen 4:25,26*), when people began to call upon the name of the Lord, God has been calling together his chosen people. He will continue to do this until the last person is saved before our Lord's return.

In the western way of thinking, great importance is placed on the fact that God chose us as individuals. The old song expresses this:

*Jesus is my Saviour, this I know,*
*He has given peace to my heart . . .*

Carried to an extreme, this is a very lonely position. It suggests that I stand alone before God, just the two of us. Peter gives a wider perspective when he writes that we are a chosen people. God calls us, but he calls us together. In every local congregation, he brings each individual together – even what we might call 'the awkward squad', or the 'in group', those who attend and those who stay away. Even the pastor or minister is called, not to be separate, but to be part of God's community, on level ground with everyone else.

My wise father used to quote the verse:

*To live above with the saints we love,*
*That will be peace and glory!*
*But to live below with the saints we*
*  know,*
*Now that's a different story!*

Living below with the saints we know is our lifetime destiny. One of the objectives of God's Salvation Project is to call together a chosen people, a people belonging to God. So let us celebrate the fact that we have been and are being chosen together in him. Let us build the kingdom of God, showing a deep, heartfelt unity with all whom Christ has given us as our brothers and sisters. Remember we cannot choose our family – our task is to love and appreciate them, and to pray for them.

# FRIDAY 14 FEBRUARY
## The Restoration of Creation

Romans 8:18–25

'And the hope is that in the end the whole of created life will be rescued from the tyranny of change and decay, and have its share in that magnificent liberty which can only belong to the children of God!' (v. 21, J. B. Phillips).

God's Salvation Project does not deal only with the salvation of humankind. His plan is also to restore the whole of creation. J. B. Phillips, in his version of this verse, speaks so clearly to my heart. 'The whole of created life will be rescued from the tyranny of change and decay.' We feel this pervasive tyranny of change affecting our everyday lives. Our entire world seems to be changing, and few of the changes seem to be for the better. None of the elements of our life are unaffected – our homes, our livelihood and even our families are all subject to this tyranny.

The change and decay in creation is causing huge problems for poor people in every part of the world. These people live on the edges of society, often garnering a livelihood from the environment around them. As industrialisation increases, these fragile livelihoods are being threatened and the powerful forces of change and decay are further impoverishing people.

God's great salvation objective is to restore creation to its former state of created goodness. There is an end to this cycle of change and decay. The clock is ticking and the end of it all is coming. This is not a vain dream. It is the reality that the Salvation Project is for a finite period of time. Then, when all has been accomplished according to God's plan, he will bring in a new heaven and new earth. That will, in Phillips' wonderful phrase, 'share in the magnificent liberty which can only belong to the children of God!'

An antidote to the confusion that change can bring comes from the words of the old hymn:

*Change and decay in all around I see;*
*O thou who changest not, abide with*
*   me!*

Henry Francis Lyte, *SASB 670*

### Prayer
*Loving God, as I stay close to you today, I am grateful that you never change. You are the rock of my life and I trust you. I await the restoration of your creation. Come quickly, Lord Jesus.*

# SATURDAY 15 FEBRUARY
## To Evaluate the Project's Effectiveness

Revelation 20:11–15

'And I saw the dead, great and small, standing before the throne, and books were opened. Another book was opened, which is the book of life. The dead were judged according to what they had done as recorded in the books' (v. 12, NIV).

A key to good project management is the keeping of accurate records. When all the activities are going on, the staff of a big project are required each month to record the results of their efforts. So many plans start off well. But, as the project progresses, not everything goes as planned. Some things succeed far better than you would have ever planned and some things simply fail.

When we are implementing community development projects around the world the most important final stage of the project is the evaluation. This is the time when the whole activity is evaluated. The donors' auditors examine the project's records. The big question always is: Have the funds we gave to this project been used correctly? The records are all important at this stage. In the same way, the Salvation Project will be evaluated according to the project records. The reading today speaks of the books being opened, books that record all our actions. The performance of each person in the Salvation Project will be subject to this final examination, and we will be judged by what we have done.

Last year I visited Kosovo and spoke to a Muslim there about this final judgment. I said to him, 'I know that you believe that Jesus will return and will judge all men and women. Don't you think that we can wait for all those who have committed such atrocities against your people to receive their just deserts at that time?' He replied, 'Yes, we Muslims believe, like you do, in the last judgment, but that day is too far away for us. We need justice here and now.'

In that statement lies the tragedy of the Balkans and of so many similar situations around the world. The day of God's justice is seen to be too far off. Yet God's word is true – in the end justice will prevail. We pray that that day may come soon.

---

*Jesus shall conquer, lift up the strain!*
*Evil shall perish and righteousness shall reign.*
*Albert Orsborn, SASB 173*

# SUNDAY 16 FEBRUARY
## The Great Story of God

Psalm 78:1–4; 56–72

'He chose David his servant . . . to be the shepherd of his people
Jacob, of Israel his inheritance' (vv. 70,71, NIV).

My grandchildren love stories. They know all about Thomas the Tank Engine. They enjoy Percy the Park Keeper. They love Hairy Maclary and his shaggy friends. But their favourite stories are the ones about themselves. 'Once upon a time there was a family with a Mummy and Daddy and lots of little boys . . .' The personal stories with familiar figures are the ones that really light up their eyes. 'Tell us again,' they say.

There is something compelling about a big story that has our own story at its centre. Psalm 78 is a story like that. It is a psalm–story of the people of God, from Zoan to Zion, as someone has called it. This story is far more than a recital of historical events. The psalmist's intent is made clear at the beginning. He is going to teach 'in parables' and utter 'hidden things, things from of old'. He wants this story to be told to every generation of God's people so that every generation will know God's sovereignty and God's sovereign claim, not simply as information, but as a life-saving hope. The object is for each generation to 'put their trust in God and . . . not forget his deeds but . . . keep his commands' (v. 7).

The psalm weaves the pattern of Israel's dark disobedience, rebellion and faithlessness, together with the bright threads of God's saving grace, miracles of provision and guidance, and his wonder–working power. Over and over again the people promised to follow God's way. Over and over again those promises proved false as they fell into sin. Yet over and over again their rebelliousness was met by God's mercy and forgiveness.

This story of the people of God is our story as well. Psalm 78 reminds us that knowledge of God's commands does not guarantee faithfulness. Like the people of Israel, we too stand day after day, year after year, generation after generation, in need of God's persistent and amazing grace.

## To reflect on
*In every era, the faith of the people of God is only one generation away from extinction.*

# MONDAY 17 FEBRUARY
## The Expulsion of Rebels from Heaven

Luke 10:17–20

'I saw Satan fall like lightning from heaven . . . However,
do not rejoice that the spirits submit to you, but rejoice that your
names are written in heaven' (vv. 18,20, NIV).

In the project format, the goal of the project is the main change in the community that the project will achieve. That main aim is divided up into different objectives. For every project objective there need to be activities that are the means to achieve the goal.

The first main objective in the Salvation Project is to destroy the rebellion. The first activity that relates to this first objective is the expulsion of rebels from heaven.

We have no book in the Bible that focuses on this, but passages in Isaiah 14:12–14, Jeremiah 4:23–26 and Ezekiel 28:11–17 describe a great battle that raged between the rebel Satan and God himself. It seems as though in this battle Satan was banished from heaven because of his rebellion.

In today's passage, Jesus speaks of that battle to his disciples. The imagery is vivid; the battle must have been immense. It is surprising that Hollywood has never tried to feature this great spectacle. It would banish *Star Wars* and *The Lord of the Rings* film series into obscurity. Or would it? The attraction of these great movie series has in fact been the cosmic battles between right and wrong. This surely resonates with something in our innate being which points to the greatest of all conflicts – when Satan was banished from heaven.

In the reading today, Jesus quickly grounds his disciples in a necessary reality when he says, 'Do not rejoice that the spirits submit to you, but rejoice that your names are written in heaven.'

We are to understand the larger heavenly aspect of the Salvation Project. But we must also keep our eyes on the important part for us, which is to ensure that we are truly saved and that our names are written in the Book of Life.

### Prayer
*Loving God, thank you that your word leads into all truth. Show me my true spiritual state today. Reassure me right now that my name is written in the Book of Life. Thank you for your reassurance, I was just checking.*

# TUESDAY 18 FEBRUARY

## To Demonstrate Obedience in a Created Being

Philippians 2:5–11

'And being found in appearance as a man, he humbled himself and became obedient to death – even death on a cross!' (v. 8, NIV).

Jesus, in shedding his glory and humbling himself and dying on earth, demonstrated that obedience was possible. This was in direct contrast to Satan's rebellion. By demonstrating this obedience, Jesus proved that it was possible to live in complete obedience to God. This gave him the power over Satan and death. We can see the contrast between Christ's way and Satan's way:

Before his fall Satan was one of God's most senior angelic beings.

As God, Jesus was always Satan's superior (v. 6).

Satan had aspirations of becoming equal with God.

Jesus 'did not consider equality with God something to be grasped' (v. 6), that is, something to be obtained by violence.

Satan wanted to make a name for himself.

Jesus 'made himself nothing' (v. 7).

Satan's pride was the reason for his fall.

Jesus' humility was the reason for his victory. 'Therefore God exalted him to the highest place' (v. 9).

The way to victory as a Christian is the opposite of Satan's way on earth. We are not to strive to beat everyone else in the rat race. Remember the winner of the rat race is always a rat. We are to follow Christ's path of humility. When God's blessing is on our life, he will lift us up. There is no need to struggle by means of our own efforts. Submission to God's way for our lives is all that is required.

## Prayer
*Loving God, help us to have Christ's attitude in all things. When we are tempted to follow the world's way, keep reminding us that Christ's way to victory is the only sure way to win God's approval.*

# WEDNESDAY 19 FEBRUARY

## Trial of the Rebels

### Matthew 25:31–45

'Come, you who are blessed by my Father; take your inheritance, the kingdom prepared for you since the creation of the world . . . I tell you the truth, whatever you did for one of the least of these brothers of mine, you did for me' (vv. 34,40, NIV).

Jesus' account of the dividing of the nations, like sheep from goats, graphically describes the finale of the rebellion. It is at this point that all the rebels receive their just deserts. However, the criterion for the judgment is disconcertingly simple. The divide will come between those who have acted in simple kindness to their fellows and those who haven't. You may ask: 'But what about theological purity, intense spirituality, high ecclesiastical position or evangelical success? Don't any of these things count?' Not according to the shepherd who will divide the sheep from the goats. So where is the catch? The answer, in breathtaking simplicity, is – there is none.

William Barclay says God will judge us according to our reaction to human need. He says such reaction will be shown in simple ways, like offering a meal to a hungry person. It must be uncalculating. The people featured in the Scripture passage did not offer help in order to earn a reward. Rather, they did it because they could not help themselves. It was the reaction of an instinctive, quite uncalculatingly loving heart.

He recounts the story of Martin of Tours, a Roman soldier and a Christian. One wintry day as Martin was entering a city, a beggar stopped him and asked for alms. Martin had no money, but the beggar was shivering with the cold, so Martin gave him what he had. He took off his soldier's coat, worn and frayed as it was, cut it in half and gave half to the beggar. That night he had a dream in which he saw angels in heaven, and Jesus in the midst of them. Jesus was wearing half of a Roman soldier's cloak. One of the angels said to him, 'Master, why are you wearing that battered old cloak?' Jesus answered softly, 'My servant Martin gave it to me.'

Today let us simply follow the teaching given. As we reach out in human kindness we may, in the process, catch a fleeting image of the face of Jesus himself in the faces of those we help.

# THURSDAY 20 FEBRUARY
## The Revelation of My Plan in Creation

Psalm 19:1–4

'The heavens declare the glory of God; the skies proclaim the work of his hands . . . There is no speech or language where their voice is not heard' (vv. 1,3, NIV).

One of the great objectives of the Salvation Project is God's intention to gather together a people who belong to him. We will discover that he reveals his special plans through the establishment of the people of Israel and then, by extension, to the whole world through his Church. But today's reading teaches of a far wider expression of God's purpose. The psalmist declares that God's nature and being are shown to all humankind by creation itself.

The psalmist says, 'There is no speech or language where their voice is not heard' (*v. 3*). This revelation of who God is, is clear to all peoples. This is inherently just. After all, how could God judge those peoples who lived far from the Middle East, who had no contact with the patriarchs, and who lived long before the missionary advance of the Church throughout the world? The answer is that through creation God has revealed enough of himself for all people everywhere to live a life that is pleasing to God. Even today, for those who have had no real encounter with the gospel in an intelligible form, the natural revelation of God is sufficient.

This revelation is not passive, for the verbs used all speak with an active declaration of who God is. God is the same to all people, he is not a God who is silent. He speaks to all whose searching hearts, quiet minds and open ears are tuned in to his voice. Whether he does this through the channel of the Church, or through his people in the world declaring his truth, or through the witness of the heavens, God speaks to all humankind.

I believe when all is revealed in Glory we will be astounded at the ways God has communicated to his people. But this is not a cop-out. God has clearly called us to be his witnesses in an active way in the world we live in. May we allow the heavens to give their silent witness, while we follow our destiny to be his vocal witnesses here on earth.

# FRIDAY 21 FEBRUARY
## The Establishment of Pilot Project Israel

Genesis 12:1–4

'Leave your country, your people and your father's household and go to the land I will show you' (v. 1, NIV).

In community development work, the goal of establishing a new pro–gramme usually begins with a small pilot project. Once the lessons of the pilot project have been learned, then the programme can be ex–panded to the wider community.

In the Salvation Project, God used this same pattern. The people of Israel were chosen to be God's pilot project. Through them the plan of salvation for all people was established. It all started with Abram – or Abraham, as he came to be called. He came onto the stage suddenly when God first promised to make him a great nation (v. 2).

Second, God promised that through him all people on earth would be blessed (v. 3). That is where we come in. The third part of the covenant took place when, as it says, 'So Abram left, as the LORD had told him' (v. 4). God's revelation was wonderful, but the covenant was sealed only when Abram obeyed.

Abraham is the father of all who believe, because he obeyed and stepped out in faith. We may wonder why God chose Abraham. The answer is found in a phrase in Nehemiah 9:8. Speaking of Abraham, the writer says: 'You found his heart faithful to you, and you made a covenant with him.'

God did not arbitrarily choose Abraham because he needed some-one and Abraham was as good as anyone else. The writer says that Abraham's heart was faithful towards God. By the silent witness of the heavens, Abraham displayed his faith. And God, who looks on the heart, saw that this was a person he could use to expand his Salvation Project.

In the same way today, God searches the hearts of all people. Those who really want to serve God are seen and recognised. We do not have to be perfect. Abraham himself was far from perfect. But when our heart's desire is to serve God, then he takes what we have and uses us in his great plan.

## Prayer
*God who searches all hearts, I want to serve you all the days of my life. Take me and use me.*

# SATURDAY 22 FEBRUARY
## Extension of the Pilot Project to the Whole World

Acts 2:36–41

'Repent and be baptised, every one of you, in the name of Jesus Christ for the forgiveness of your sins. And you will receive the gift of the Holy Spirit. The promise is for you and your children and for all who are far off – for all whom the Lord our God will call' (v. 38, NIV).

In community development, pilot projects seem small and insignificant. A great deal of effort is taken in the early stages to ensure that all the problems are worked on. Then, when the extension project starts, something wonderful happens. Suddenly everyone sees the changes that community development can bring and they begin to get excited. In the same way the Church, when it came into being by wind and fire, transformed and is still transforming the world. On the Day of Pentecost the Salvation Project changed from being the small pilot project that God was working out with the children of Abraham to a worldwide concern.

In these verses we see the transition happening. Peter said, 'The promise is for you and your children.' Here he is speaking to the Jews in Jerusalem, who saw themselves as the children of the promise. God had promised their father Abraham that they would be his people. The recent movement of Jews who recognise that Jesus is Messiah is a continuation of this promise.

But the extension project follows, '. . . and for all who are far off – for all whom the Lord our God will call'. This promise covers us all. Geographically we are far off from the land of Israel, but this promise covers every land. Generationally we are far off, as it is almost seventy generations since Peter gave this promise. Spiritually we are far off, because of our need for repentance from sin.

The promise is that if we repent and are baptised – that is, if we identify ourselves with God and his people – then we will receive the gift of the Holy Spirit.

### Prayer
*Father, as we prepare our hearts for Easter, let your Spirit come as a wind and blow out all the debris that has collected within us. May the Spirit's fire warm us again so that you can reveal yourself to us in a new way. As we walk through Easter, following the steps of Jesus, teach us again the wonder of your salvation.*

# SUNDAY 23 FEBRUARY
## A Prayer for Desperate Times

Psalm 79

'Help us, O God our Saviour, for the glory of your name;
deliver us and forgive our sins for your name's sake' (v. 9, NIV).

This psalm is believed to have been written at the time of the destruction of Jerusalem and the temple in 587 BC. This incident was a defining moment for the people of Israel, changing their lives for ever. Many people were killed, many others taken into captivity. The people of Israel lost their homes and their symbols of national stability and security. Even worse than the physical destruction was a sense of the loss of God's protection and care. They had seen themselves as God's chosen people, immune to disaster, certain that David's dynasty would never fail. The destruction of the nation was therefore a theological crisis as well as a political, economic and social one. Psalm 79 is the psalmist's attempt, on behalf of the people, to respond with a heart of faith to the events that have wrecked their lives.

Prayer in the midst of tragedy has no time to dress itself in fine language. This is real prayer from the gut, an honest and desperate plea for God to show himself to be the God whom the people had always known, the God of their salvation. They have been reduced to nothing. Comfortable faith has been shattered along with everything else. In spite of this, they do not give in to their neighbours' mocking taunts to deny God's existence. In the midst of their loss and chaos, they hold on to their faith like a rescue rope that passes from one person to another.

Full of anguish at the unspeakable things the people have seen, and anger at those responsible, the psalmist tells God exactly what is in their hearts. Yet even in their cry for vengeance, it is God's action they want. In spite of the present tragedy, they believe that God's delivering power in the past will be seen once more in the future. Holding firmly to that rope of faith, they pledge themselves, yet again, to praise him.

## To reflect on
*This psalm is indeed a prayer for today. It is recited every Friday afternoon at the Wailing Wall at the temple in Jerusalem.*

# HOSEA – GOD'S LOVE STORY

## Introduction

The book of Hosea is full of striking imagery. The prophet describes the nation of Israel as a sick person, a grapevine, an olive tree, a woman in labour, an oven, morning mist, chaff and smoke. He describes God as a father, lion, leopard, mother bear, dew and rain. But the most powerful image of all is that God is like a husband who loves and keeps on loving a wife, even when she is persistently unfaithful to him. Hosea's story and God's story weave together, making the prophet not only the voice, but also the living illustration of God's love.

G. Campbell Morgan described the person Hosea as 'a sob and sigh and song merging in a name'. It is God's sob and sigh that Hosea bears, and God's song of love that he sings to the nation of Israel.

This love story is also a story of judgment and a story with a call to choose carefully. Even though Israel kept on choosing death rather than life, rebellion rather than righteousness, God kept on loving the people to whom he had bound himself in covenant love. In the reading of Hosea's story over the next two weeks, may you discover that this love story, with its invitation, is written with you, too, in mind.

> Sow for yourselves righteousness, reap the fruit of unfailing love, and break up your unploughed ground; for it is time to seek the LORD, until he comes and showers righteousness on you (10:12).

# MONDAY 24 FEBRUARY

## A Love Story

### Hosea 1:1–2:1

'When the LORD began to speak through Hosea, the LORD said to him, "Go, take to yourself an adulterous wife and children of unfaithfulness, because the land is guilty of the vilest adultery in departing from the LORD" ' (v. 2, NIV).

How do you describe something so big, so high, so deep, and so wide, that words just cannot reach around it? How do you describe the indescribable? How do you teach a person about God when the person's world is water and sand and trees? One way is to tell a story, which is what Hosea did: God is like a man who loved a woman so much that he never gave up loving her, even though she was unfaithful to him.

Hosea was a prophet to the northern kingdom of Israel at a dark time in the nation's history. Israel's last six kings were wicked rulers. They imposed heavy taxes, they oppressed the poor, they encouraged the worship of idols and disregarded the God of Moses and Abraham. Against this backdrop of national unfaithfulness, Hosea had a personal story of unfaithfulness to tell.

Hosea married a woman named Gomer. Following the marriage, three children were born to them – Jezreel, Lo–Ruhamah and Lo–Ammi – symbolic, sorrowful names.

Gomer was unfaithful to Hosea, chasing after other lovers. But instead of abandoning her, Hosea bought her back from slavery and restored her as his wife. That's the story. The first part is tragic but not unusual. The second part is most unusual.

Hosea has been called the prophet of the broken heart. Through his own personal tragedy, he came to understand the heart of God, and what God suffered when his people sinned. Some theologians have written about the 'impassive' nature of God, claiming that God is incapable of real suffering. But if that is so, then the book of Hosea needs to be rewritten.

God suffers in the presence of sin, but his love is such that he will find a way for the sinner to come home, a way of release, a way of ransom, a way of rescue. If you are unsure of that, then check out the story of the Good Samaritan (*Luke 10:30–37*), or the story of the lost sheep (*Luke 15:4–7*). If you are still unconvinced, then take a long, lingering look at the cross of Calvary.

# TUESDAY 25 FEBRUARY
## A Door of Hope

Hosea 2:2–23

'There I will give her back her vineyards, and will make the Valley of Achor a door of hope' (v. 15, NIV).

In spite of Gomer's unfaithfulness, Hosea was still faithful. In spite of Israel's unfaithfulness, God was still faithful. The parallel stories weave together in this chapter as judgment gives way to punishment, which gives way to restoration.

The adulterous woman was brought to trial and found guilty. Just as Hosea provided Gomer with clothing, so God provided the children of Israel with plenty of rain for their crops, food and water, wood, linen and oil. But Israel ignored God and worshipped Baal, the Canaanite god who was believed to control the weather and the fertility of the land.

In sadness as much as in anger, God determined to hedge Israel in, to isolate her, and to make the rewards of idol worship so disappointing that the people would be persuaded to turn back to God. Exposed to public shame, Israel would discover that Baal was powerless to help.

Suddenly the language of punishment and severity gives way to the language of tenderness and restoration. 'I am now going to allure her; I will lead her into the desert and speak tenderly to her. There I . . . will make the Valley of Achor a door of hope.' The Valley of Achor ('trouble') was the place where Achan sinned by keeping forbidden war treasures (*Josh* 7).

In the desert, far away from Canaan's tempting idols, God promised to take the things that had troubled the nation and to open a door of hope. Gomer, the nation of Israel, will say, 'I will return to my husband.' In that day, God will no longer be like a master or owner ('Baal'), he will be like a husband. The bride price that God will pay will be righteousness, justice, love, compassion and faithfulness. Even Gomer's children will be renamed. Punishment and abandonment will give way to the fresh beginning of a new covenant relationship with God. The people will be his people and he will be their God. These words show the heart of a loving God laid bare.

## To reflect on
*It was her reform, not her riddance, that God wanted.*

# WEDNESDAY 26 FEBRUARY
## Redemption and Return

### Hosea 3:1–5

'The LORD said to me, "Go, show your love to your wife again, though she is loved by another and is an adulteress. Love her as the LORD loves the Israelites, though they turn to other gods" ' (v. 1, NIV).

Hosea now picks up the narrative of his own story. The Lord speaks to him, telling him to love his wife again, even though she is unfaithful to him. In Gomer's story, the people of Israel will also see their own story.

In obedience to God's initiative and instructions, Hosea has first of all to buy her back from the slavery and prostitution into which she has sold herself. He pays fifteen shekels of silver and a homer and a lethek of barley. The usual price for a slave was thirty shekels of silver. This amount of barley was a slave's food for the day. So low has Gomer sunk that Hosea gets her back for half price and a day's ration.

Hosea's love, like the love of God, is not selfish, revengeful or be-grudging. As Paul adds later, it is not rude, nor self-seeking, it keeps no record of wrongs, but always protects, always hopes, always per-severes (see *1 Cor 13:5,7*). Armed with such love, Hosea buys Gomer back and brings her home where he commits himself to live with her and to look after her.

The restoration of the relation-ship between Hosea and Gomer is parallel to the restoration between God and Israel. There is no mention of punishment, only of Israel living for many days without all those things that led them astray and away from God. Israel's unworthy political leaders and religious prac-tices – 'sacrifice . . . sacred stones . . . ephod . . . idol' – that destroyed the nation's relationship with God will be removed. Then 'in the last days' the covenant relationship between God and Israel will be restored.

The parallels are clear. An adult-erous, unrepentant woman who rejects her husband and turns to other lovers is bought back and brought back to her husband. An adulterous, unrepentant nation who rejects her covenant and turns to other masters will be bought back and brought back to her God. Rejection and rebellion are met by redemption and restoration.

### To reflect on
*Somewhere between Gomer's story and Israel's story, your story of rebellion and redemption is also told.*

# THURSDAY 27 FEBRUARY
## God's Charge against Israel

### Hosea 4:1–12

'Hear the word of the LORD, you Israelites, because the
LORD has a charge to bring against you who live in the land: "There is
no faithfulness, no love, no acknowledgment of God in the land" '
(v. 1, NIV).

The story of Hosea's wayward wife now moves to the story of God's wayward people. Gomer is not mentioned again. The opening words of this chapter introduce the rest of the book.

The scene is a court of law. God, the prosecutor, has a charge to bring against his people. He has looked for faithfulness (that is, common honesty and reliability), love (that is, steadfast kindness and loyalty), and acknowledgment of God. On every count the people are found wanting. Rampant wickedness stalks through the land. A dark catalogue of sins has turned the hearts of the people away from God and poisoned the land.

Responsibility for the disobedience and waywardness of the people is laid squarely on the priests. The religious leaders have failed in their task of turning the people to God. Instead, they have encouraged the people to sin, knowing that for every sin offering that is brought, the priests will receive a portion. They have grown fat on the people's sins, relishing their wickedness. Their failure and neglect are unforgivable. God will reject them and

their families, just as they have rejected him.

In this vacuum of knowledge of God, ritual prostitution has replaced true worship. The whole nation has gone astray, selling their souls and their bodies to the Canaanite fertility gods. There is nothing God can do but leave them to wallow in their shameful ways.

What is the tone of this passage? Anger and condemnation, certainly, but that is not all. There is also the cry of rejected love, the anguish and sadness of God for his shepherds who, instead of feeding the flock, are fleecing them. There is the heartache of God for his wayward people who have turned their backs on the only One who can give them life. 'A whirlwind will sweep them away,' says Hosea. But, thank God, this is not his final word.

---

## To reflect on

*'O eternal, infinite God! You have fallen in love with what you have made! You clothed yourself in our humanity, and nearer than that you could not have come.'*

**Catherine of Siena**

# FRIDAY 28 FEBRUARY
## Judgment and Punishment

<u>Hosea 5:1–6:3</u>

'Come, let us return to the LORD. He has torn us to pieces
but he will heal us; he has injured us but he will bind up our wounds'
(6:1, NIV).

The charges against Israel in Hosea 4 lead on to judgment and punishment in the next chapter. It is not just the priests who are under fire. Both religious and political leaders have led the nation astray. Instead of providing safe guidelines for living, the leaders have spread nets and snares to trap innocent people. God says he will discipline and deal harshly with the leaders for their actions. So neglectful have been the priests that a spirit of prostitution is in the hearts of the people, making it almost impossible for them to return to God and know him as their covenant partner.

Arrogant, defiant and unfaithful, the people are headed for destruction and judgment. A trumpet declaring war is sounded. Hosea uses powerful images to describe what will happen. Instead of healing them, God will let his people be like an injured soldier whose wounds are festering with terrible infection. Changing the image, Hosea says that God will be like a lion who tears his prey to pieces and carries off what remains. Assyria may be the means of

bringing Israel and Judah to defeat, but God's verdict of punishment will be a much more fearful thing.

These dark and terrible warnings of God through Hosea, his spokesman, must have been an overwhelming weight for the prophet. His was no sticking-plaster task as he tried to tend the open festering wound of his people's rebellion. He longs for them to return to God and be restored. 'Come, let us return to the LORD,' he pleads.

Hosea must know that it will take a mighty miracle of human confession and divine grace for God to revive and restore his people. But he is sure that if they do their part in returning, acknowledging and living in God's presence, then God will do his part. As surely as the coming of the new day's sun or the winter rains, God will come to the aid of his broken people.

---

*Pray today for the spokespeople and servants of God who carry the weight of people's sins and needs before him.*

# SATURDAY 1 MARCH
## An Unrepentant People

Hosea 6:4–7:2

'For I desire mercy, not sacrifice, and acknowledgment of God rather than burnt offerings' (v. 6, NIV).

In spite of God's longing for his people, and in spite of Hosea's heartfelt pleading for them to return, the people of Israel do not turn. They do not regret or repent. They do not understand how deep and dark their sins are and how much they need the mercy and forgiveness of God. They think God's wrath will last only a few days. Little do they know that their nation will soon be taken into exile.

Called by the prophet Hosea, the people gather for a public fast of repentance. They know that God is the cause of their military defeat and that Assyria is merely the instrument of God's punishment. But they want easy repentance and cheap grace.

God replies to Israel's arrogance, not in anger, but in agonised love. 'What can I do with you?' he asks. He is like a weary parent with a defiant child. Punishment has not changed them; judgment has not brought them any closer to repentance. Their profession of loyalty is like morning dew that has no substance and disappears quickly. They say they will seek God and worship him, but in no time they are inquiring of Baal and depending on military power instead of on God. They do not seem to know what loyalty means.

God has sent them a long line of prophets – Samuel, Elijah, Elisha, Amos, Isaiah and others – to declare God's word and to warn of his punishment. But instead of turning to God in love, obedience and worship, the people continue with their religious rituals, then do as they please.

What God wants is mercy (*hesed* – covenant loyalty) and not daily sacrifices. He wants them to know him, rather than giving him their burnt offerings. God is like a husband who longs for his wife Israel's heart, bound to him in trust and love and faithfulness. No sacrifice, no ritual repentance can substitute for that intimate relationship.

## To reflect on
*If God had a choice between your 'doing' (your performance, programme and practices) and your 'being', which would he choose? Check out 1 Samuel 16:7.*

# SUNDAY 2 MARCH
## Make Your Face Shine upon Us

Psalm 80

'Restore us, O LORD God Almighty; make your face shine upon us, that we may be saved' (v. 19, NIV).

Psalm 80 is a sorrowful prayer. The psalmist, Asaph, addresses God as 'Shepherd of Israel', the only time in the Old Testament that he is addressed in this way, although the image of shepherd was a familiar one. As the aged patriarch Israel gave his blessing to his son Joseph, he spoke of the unfailing goodness of God 'who has been my shepherd all my life to this day' (*Gen 48:15*). In Psalm 23 David addressed God as Jehovah–Rohi, 'my shepherd', as he declared God's unfailing love and protection.

The sorrow of Psalm 80 has come about because the Shepherd of Israel who once cared for his people seems to have failed them now. Using human terms to describe the indescribable, the psalmist suggests that God their shepherd has done the unthinkable and gone to sleep, leaving his people to the mercy of their enemies. Instead of the green pastures and quiet waters of Psalm 23, tears have been their food. Their once protective shepherd has turned angry.

Urging God to arouse himself and come to their aid, the psalmist cries out with a refrain that grows in intensity throughout the psalm. 'Restore us, O God, make your face shine upon us, that we may be saved.' The word 'restore' is from the Hebrew word 'turn', and so their prayer is, 'Turn us again. Let your face once again smile on us with favour and kindness' (cf. *Num 6:25*).

Using another tender image, the psalmist writes of Israel as a vine that God took from Egypt and planted in his land. There the vine spread and grew, filling the whole land and covering mountains and mighty cedars with its shade. But now the great vine is broken down, uprooted by wild boars and trampled by passers–by who plunder its fruit.

Once again this is desperate prayer for those desperate times when the familiar, comforting ways of God seem to let us down, leaving us exposed and vulnerable. In such times of sorrow, there is nowhere else to turn. God may be the problem, but he is also the only solution.

# MONDAY 3 MARCH
## A Sad, Sad Story

Hosea 9:10–17

'When I found Israel, it was like finding grapes in the desert; when I saw your fathers, it was like seeing the early fruit on the fig-tree. But when they came to Baal Peor, they consecrated themselves to that shameful idol and became as vile as the thing they loved' (v. 10, NIV).

In spite of God's judgments and repeated attempts to call his people back, Israel steadfastly refused to turn back and seek God. Instead of looking to God for help, she turned to alliances with foreign nations. Hosea seems almost lost for words to describe the full extent of Israel's idolatry and sin, her rejection, violence, deceit, betrayal, robbery and arrogance. He uses striking, shocking images to paint a picture of a nation that has lost its way.

The leaders of Israel are 'adulterers, burning like an oven' (7:4). They are full of lust for power and are like a careless baker who neglects his responsibilities. Israel is like 'a flat cake not turned over' (7:8). Unwise policies and foreign allegiances have left the people useless and wasted.

Israel is like 'a dove, easily deceived and senseless' (7:11). Instead of being consistently loyal to God, she is making alliances, now with Egypt, now with Assyria. Israel is like 'a faulty bow' (7:16). Shot from a twisted bow, Israel has missed the mark (the picture behind the word 'sin'), and serves other gods.

Israel is 'swallowed up ... like a worthless thing' (8:8). She who was once chosen by God has now lost her special identity and become worthless. Israel sows the wind and reaps the whirlwind (8:7). This agricultural proverb sums up what Israel has done and what every farmer knows, that a harvest is directly related to what is planted.

The tragedy is that Israel was once like a new bride, full of glorious promise. God said that when he found her, it was 'like finding grapes in the desert ... like seeing the early fruit on the fig-tree' (9:10). But in turning away from God and consecrating herself to idols, Israel has prostituted her glory, wasted her inheritance, abandoned her special calling. Instead of the fullness of promise, Israel has become barren and blighted. With deep sadness Hosea concludes, 'My God will reject them because they have not obeyed him; they will be wanderers among the nations' (9:17). Is there no hope for Israel?

# TUESDAY 4 MARCH
## Break Up Your Unploughed Ground

Hosea 10:1–15

'Sow for yourselves righteousness, reap the fruit of unfailing love, and break up your unploughed ground; for it is time to seek the LORD, until he comes and showers righteousness on you' (v. 12, NIV).

Hosea uses two further images to describe Israel's unfaithfulness. He says she was 'a spreading vine' (v. 1). Under the reign of Jeroboam II, Israel gained military and economic strength, but the more prosperous the nation became, the more it lavished on idols. Israel was 'a trained heifer' (v. 11), strong and hard-working, brought into God's service. But instead of sowing righteousness and reaping the blessings of God's unfailing covenant love, Israel planted unrighteous seeds and reaped the consequence – the poisonous fruit of her own deception.

Hosea pauses to call the people back to God, back to faithfulness and fruitfulness. 'Sow ... reap ... break up your unploughed ground.' His words are surely a call to believers in our day as well. Is there a message here for those times when, like Israel, our fields fall barren?

A spiritual drought exposes our need for God. Brought to the end of ourselves, we may discover that we have lost our mindfulness of God. 'Things fall apart; the centre cannot hold' (W. B. Yeats). When things at the centre of our lives fragment, we are reminded that God has made us for himself and that, left to ourselves, we can do nothing.

Awareness of our need may awaken us to a new longing for God. When the ground is parched, nothing matters but rain. When our souls are parched, nothing matters but God. 'My soul thirsts for God, for the living God,' cried the psalmist (Ps 42:2).

A spiritual drought may restore our fruitfulness for God. Wheat growers know that a wheat field will yield four or five times what is sown. But after several years of planting in the same field, the yield gradually drops. When a field lies fallow for a year and is then ploughed and replanted, the yield jumps to twice the normal level, producing eight to ten bushels of wheat for every bushel sown. So it is with our souls.

*Forgive, O Lord, my heart untended*
*Bring fire into this night just ended.*
*Fan to flame my heart fresh-rended*
*Spirit, make your mark.*
*David Henderson*

# WEDNESDAY 5 MARCH

## God of Compassion

Hosea 11:1–11

'How can I give you up, Ephraim? How can I hand you over, Israel? . . . My heart is changed within me; all my compassion is aroused' (v. 8, NIV).

In the final chapters of his book, Hosea writes with powerful word pictures of God's intense and unfailing love for Israel. Hosea, the betrayed husband, has written of God's husbandly love being betrayed. Now the images become even more tender as God speaks of his love for Israel in the past, and his hope for her future.

God likens his care to that of a father teaching his child how to walk. 'I loved him . . . I . . . taught Ephraim [Israel] to walk, taking them by the arms.' God was like a nurse, 'I . . . healed them.' He was like a husband, 'I led them with cords of human kindness, with ties of love.' He was like a herdsman caring for cattle at the end of a day's hard work. 'I lifted the yoke from their neck and bent down to feed them.'

How was such strong and tender love responded to? Four statements tell Israel's story. 'They went from me . . . they did not realise it was I . . . they refuse to repent . . . my people are determined to turn from me.' God was the persistent, faithful Lover, but his people turned and spurned that love, stubbornly, rebelliously, ungratefully.

What then is to be done? Pause for a moment on this holy ground in the book of Hosea and ask yourself what you would do if you were God. Humanly speaking, the laws of tough love say there is nothing to do but give them up, abandon them to the consequences of their deliberate sin.

But God's answer comes, 'I am God, and not man . . . How can I give you up? . . . I will not . . . I will not . . . I will not.' What holds God back from abandoning Israel? Not something in Israel, for sure, but something in God himself. The far-seeing God sees potential and possibilities within her that even Israel herself cannot see.

### To reflect on

*This God of compassion, in whom sorrow and love mingle together, declared that he would never give up his people. Hear him say the same thing to you today.*

# THURSDAY 6 MARCH
## Rejection and Redemption

Hosea 13:1–16

'I will ransom them from the power of the grave;
I will redeem them from death' (v. 14, NIV).

This chapter of Hosea comes with a sudden jarring after the previous chapter with its tender images of the God who will not give up his beloved people. Hosea once more laments the lies and deceitfulness of Israel in her relationship with God. But now God is like an exasperated parent who suddenly cries, 'Enough!'

God reviews his gracious acts in the past, reminding Israel of who he is and what he has done. 'I am the LORD your God, who brought you out of Egypt' (12:9) . . . 'I spoke to the prophets' (12:10) . . . 'I cared for you in the desert' (13:5) . . . 'I fed them' (13:6). If God had not brought his chosen people out of slavery in Egypt, and if he had not miraculously provided for them time and time again in the burning heat of the Sinai Desert, they would not have survived. But at every point they took God's gifts, then turned their backs. They put idols made of silver in the place of the living God. His provision made them proud. His faithfulness made them forget.

In a series of terrible 'I will' statements, God declares that he will now turn against his people. He will no longer reach out to them in tender love, but will deliberately act like a vicious lion or leopard, or like an angry mother bear robbed of her cubs. Israel will be savagely ripped apart and torn limb from limb. Israel will be like a baby in the womb that does not come to birth (13:13). Israel will be like a land parched with drought (13:15). Israel will be slaughtered in war (13:16).

These dreadful predictions are hard to read alongside the tender imagery of the previous chapter. But through one verse a light of resurrection hope shines brightly. God says, 'I will ransom them from the power of the grave; I will redeem them from death' (v. 14). The nation may be headed for defeat, but even death will not thwart God or his plans. God's final word has not yet been spoken.

# FRIDAY 7 MARCH
## You Choose!

### Hosea 14:1–3

'Assyria cannot save us; we will not mount war-horses. We will never again say "Our gods" to what our own hands have made, for in you the fatherless find compassion' (v. 3, NIV).

Hosea's book concludes with a life-determining choice. He gives yet again an appeal for repentance (see 10:12, 12:6). Throughout his story, Hosea has laid before the people of Israel the ways of life and death, of God's favour and of God's punishment. He himself has been a living illustration of a love that will not let go. But he knows, just as any preacher knows, that ultimately the choice of how one lives is an individual one.

Hosea describes the way of repentance in these few verses. Then in the last part of the chapter he describes the promise of restoration, the response that God gives to those who turn to him. Repentance is more than a formula to follow. Repentance is like what happens when someone is walking in one direction, then stops, turns and walks back in the direction from which they came. Hosea sums it up in two imperatives – 'Return ... take words with you.'

'Turn back, nation of Israel,' Hosea calls. As a nation in the desert after the escape from Egypt, they had encountered the living, covenant-making God. They had pledged themselves to be his people and to follow his commands. But through generations of turning away, they lost their way, stumbled and fell into sin. Now you must turn back, he says, from the things that have led you astray – the idolatrous relationships with other gods, and the alliances you have made with foreign powers.

As you turn, take words with you, words of confession, words that tell your sin-story, words that cast you upon the mercy and forgiveness of God. He is the only one in whom a fatherless, vulnerable, undeserving nation can find help and compassion. Only in him can 'solid joys and lasting treasure' (*SASB 157*) be found.

## To reflect on
*At holiday times, when my children were young, we would have 'choosing days' on which we would take turns to decide where to go, what to have for meals and so on. Thinking of Hosea's call to repentance, let today be a 'choosing day' for you.*

# SATURDAY 8 MARCH
## The Promise of Restoration

Hosea 14:4–9

'O Ephraim, what more have I to do with idols? I will answer him and care for him. I am like a green pine tree; your fruitfulness comes from me' (v. 8, NIV).

The book of Hosea is like a tree seen in all its seasons – from the winter bleakness of a nation stripped of its blessings to the promise of abundant fruitfulness for a nation that repents and returns to her God.

Here God speaks, simply, persuasively, with words full of grace and unfailing, persistent love. When God's people return to him and worship only him, God promises his healing and forgiveness. His undeserved love is a free expression of divine commitment, a God-sized love that will never let his people go.

Once the problem of sin is dealt with (v. 4), God will bless his people. In contrast to the fierce images of God in the previous chapter, where he was pictured as 'a lion ... a leopard ... a bear robbed of her cubs', here he is described as 'the dew to Israel'. This is not the passing morning mist of Israel's shallow repentance (see 6:4), but a symbol of God's daily blessing. Just as dew brings life-giving moisture to plants in the dry summer months, so the divine life will nourish and transform God's people.

They will be like a beautiful, fragrant lily, and be as strong and enduring as the towering cedars of Lebanon. The people of Israel will be like a plant with deep roots that cannot be destroyed. In the shade of this great tree, multitudes will find shelter. The nation will be as fruitful as a bountiful grain field, a blossoming grapevine and the famed wine of Lebanon. These are all pictures of God's rich blessing on the nation. Instead of bringing drought and death, God will lovingly give his returning people the covenant blessings he promised long ago.

Then, for the only time in the Old Testament, God himself is likened to a tree. To his people Israel, called here Ephraim (meaning 'fruitful'), he says, 'I am like a green pine tree; your fruitfulness comes from me.' God alone can turn death into life, a dry land into a flourishing garden. Only his powerful love can change people and transform his world.

# SUNDAY 9 MARCH
## Rejoice and Remember

### Psalm 81

'Sing for joy to God our strength; shout aloud to the God of Jacob!'
(v. 1, NIV).

After a series of bleak psalms, Psalm 81 stands in contrast as a song of celebration. This festival psalm was probably used for the Feast of Tabernacles, a seven-day autumn festival that recalled God's care for his people during their desert wanderings (see *Lev 23:42–43*). It also served as a feast of thanksgiving for the harvest (see *Deut 16:13–15*), and marked the conclusion of the annual cycle of religious festivals that began six months earlier with Passover and Unleavened Bread (see *Exod 23:14–17*). These religious festivals, like Easter, Pentecost and Advent in our day, were more than times of holiday and celebration. They were an opportunity to tell God's salvation story once again.

A Levite, speaking prophetically on behalf of God, calls the people of Israel to rejoice on this special occasion with musical instruments – the tambourine, harp, lyre and ram's horn. He then calls them to remember how God freed them from oppression in Egypt. With strong images of release, the psalmist describes how God 'removed the burden from their shoulders', 'set free', 'rescued' and then 'tested' them. God did more than send them out from Egypt. He accompanied them by fire and cloud in all their wanderings and taught them on the way. Theirs was an education by encounter.

The psalmist reminds them of God's call, using words that echo earlier parts of the Old Testament – the Shema and the Ten Commandments. But instead of a stern lecture about their sin and its consequences, the psalmist speaks of God's affectionate longing for his people. 'Open wide your mouth and I will fill it' . . . 'If my people would but listen' . . . 'You would be fed' . . . 'I would satisfy you.'

These verses lay bare the heart of a God of love and grace whose mercies are indeed 'new every morning' (*Lam 3:22–23*). This God who fed his people 'with the fruit of the fields, with honey from the rock and with oil from the flinty crag' (*Deut 32:13*), longs to do it again.

*Today, may your reflection and remembering lead you to rejoice and recommit.*

# WHEN PRAYER IS HARD
## Introduction

At times, the journey of prayer takes us along a gentle sunlit slope with great views of God's goodness and blessing. We sense his presence near, there's a refrain of gratitude in our heart and prayer is a delight. Answers come almost before we ask, and we feel strong and confident. This Christian walk is surely the best thing this side of heaven.

Then there are other times when, for unknown reasons, we get plunged into the deep valleys of 'Why' and 'What is happening?' and 'Where are you, God?' The straight path twists into a roundabout trail where we no longer see the way ahead. Prayer gets a 'no' answer or, even worse, God is silent. He seems to have disappeared altogether. We feel fragile, vulnerable, broken. In those moments we wonder, have we offended God? Said something to upset him?

Is there a reason for those bleak times when prayer is hard and God does not return our call? Is God doing something to mature us, grow us up? Is he teaching us to walk by faith, rather than by feelings? Are these bleak, abandoned moments my fault, the result of my sin, or are they the common lot of every sincere pray-er?

This series on prayer in the hard times will explore some of these deep and difficult questions.

# MONDAY 10 MARCH
## When God Takes His Leave

Exodus 33:1–14

'The LORD would speak to Moses face to face,
as a man speaks with his friend' (v. 11, NIV).

The Celtic people had a way of describing those places where the presence of God seems especially close. They called them 'thin places'. The prophet Isaiah met God one day in the thin place of the temple. He saw the Lord 'seated on a throne, high and exalted' (*Isa 6:1*); he heard the seraphs' song of 'Holy, holy'; he felt the building shake; he smelt the smoke that filled the temple; he tasted the burning coal on his lips. In that thin place of encounter, every sense was engaged and Isaiah emerged from the temple a different person, a man with a commission.

Moses also met God in some thin places. A common bush, way out in the desert near Horeb, was a thin place where God revealed his glory to Moses. After the children of Israel left Egypt, Moses' tent became another thin place, a venue where God would meet regularly with Moses and speak to him 'face to face'. There were no barriers between them, just the openness and intimacy of friends conversing.

As a result of the persistent sinning of the people, however, God told Moses that he would not accompany them into the promised land. At that terrible news, the people mourned. The presence of God had been constantly with them on their journey from slavery to freedom. Once again Moses pleaded with God on their behalf. 'It's your presence, God, that makes us the people we are,' said Moses. 'We are the people of the thin place. If you do not come with us, then we are lost.' And the Lord relented and replied, 'My Presence will go with you, and I will give you rest' (*v. 14*).

If you have known the thin place of God's presence in your journey of faith you will know also the heavy fog-like times of absence when God seems to have departed. It is the very memory of his presence that makes the pain of his absence so much greater.

---

*'When God seems most absent from us, he may be doing his most important work in us.'*

***Larry Crabb***

# TUESDAY 11 MARCH

## When God Says 'No'

James 4:1–3

'When you ask, you do not receive, because you ask with wrong motives, that you may spend what you get on your pleasures' (v. 3, NIV).

It seems that God gives us one of three answers when we pray. There's the 'yes' answer, which is like a green traffic light telling us to go ahead. There's the 'no' answer, which is the red light telling us to stop, and there's the orange light, which tells us to wait.

God's 'no' answers do not always make sense. We can be sure that we are asking 'in Jesus' name' and 'according to his will' but, for what-ever reason, the door stays shut, there is nothing but silence, and the answer is clearly 'no'.

Tony Campolo says that some-times we don't get what we want, so that God can give us what we need. He tells of watching the film *Hopalong Cassidy* when he was nine years old. He decided that he wanted to be a cowboy when he grew up, so he begged his father to buy him a horse. But his father refused. What would have hap-pened, Campolo wondered if, at eighteen when he was ready to go to college, his father had said, 'Sorry, son, you cannot go. We spent your college money on buying that horse for you when you were nine!'

Campolo concludes, 'My father knew what was best for me, just as the heavenly father does.'

James says that we do not receive because we pray wrongly. 'You're spoiled children, each wanting your own way' (*v. 3, The Message*). We are like a child in a toyshop just before Christmas, saying, 'Mummy, I need this.' Mummy says 'no', and a few minutes later from another part of the shop, the child says, 'Mummy, I really need this.'

We are like children standing next to the window, our noses pressed up against the glass. All we can see is what is immediately in front of us. But God, who loves us unconditionally and knows what is best for us, stands behind and beyond and sees the big picture of our lives. There are times when, for his own best reasons, God has to say 'no'. This may well be an answer full of grace.

# WEDNESDAY 12 MARCH
## When God is Silent

Psalm 42

'I say to God my Rock, "Why have you forgotten me?" ' (v. 9, NIV).

In Antarctica there are four months of the year when it is dark for twenty-four hours every day. Last year I heard a reporter there saying, 'We saw the sun on 20 April and we will not see it again until 20 August.'

There are times when prayer feels like that and we say, 'I can only just remember when God last spoke to me, or when I last felt close to him. When will he ever return?' The darkness of bereavement or illness, depression, joblessness or a broken relationship can be overwhelming. In such moments, we fear that the darkness of God's silence may be permanent.

C. S. Lewis described this feeling following the death of his wife.

When you are happy, so happy that you have no sense of need-ing him . . . you will be – or so it feels – welcomed with open arms. But go to him when your need is desperate, when all other help is vain, and what do you find? A door slammed in your face, and a sound of bolting and double bolting on the inside. After that, silence. You may as well turn away. The longer you wait, the more emphatic the silence will become. There are no lights in the windows. It might be an empty house. Was it ever inhabited? (*A Grief Observed*)

The psalmist knew this experience, too. Longing for God's presence, he met with silence from God and taunting from his enemies. 'My tears have been my food day and night, while men say to me all day long, "Where is your God?" ' (*v. 3*). Job, too, was a victim of God's silence. 'If I go to the east, he is not there; if I go to the west, I do not find him' (*Job 23:8*).

C. S. Lewis described how he hung on with courage, but initially without hope. Gradually he found grace to continue his silent journey through the dark night, believing that one day the sun would shine again.

## To reflect on
*'No matter how deep our darkness, God is deeper still.'*

**Corrie ten Boom**

# THURSDAY 13 MARCH
## When I Look for a Rainbow in the Rain

Romans 8:28–39

'For I am convinced that neither death nor life . . . neither the
present nor the future . . . nor anything else in all creation,
will be able to separate us from the love of God that is in
Christ Jesus our Lord' (vv. 38,39, NIV).

There's a song I want to have sung at my funeral. The words of 'O Love that wilt not let me go' came out of an ordinary man's deep anguish. George Matheson, the songwriter, was born in Scotland in 1842. From a young age he had trouble with failing sight and by the time he was eighteen he was totally blind. In spite of his disability, he was a brilliant student. He earned a doctorate at Edinburgh University and became an eminent preacher and writer.

When his fiancée learned that his sight was irreparably gone she refused to marry him. Out of that experience of rejection, George Matheson wrote of a love that would never fail to keep its arms around him. Out of physical blindness, his own 'flickering torch', he wrote of the light, God's sunshine blaze, that never failed to illumine his way. Out of his own suffering he wrote of joy that, like a rainbow in the rain, held a hope–filled promise before him.

In my life of faith there are times when God seems silent or, worse, absent altogether. Times when I long for a 'yes' and get a resounding 'no' to my prayers. Times when I feel rejected or abandoned. Times when it seems that I can scarcely hold on. In such moments, I need to know that I am held by a love that has not in the past, cannot in the present and will not in the future let me go. I need to discover, as George Matheson did, that even on the darkest day there is still a rainbow to be traced in the rain.

I don't know what song my parents sang to welcome me into this world, but this is the song that I want to accompany my departure:

*O Joy that seekest me through pain,*
*I cannot close my heart to thee;*
*I trace the rainbow through the rain*
*And feel the promise is not vain,*
*That morn shall tearless be.*

George Matheson, *SASB* 621

# FRIDAY 14 MARCH
## When I'm in a Desert Place

Luke 4:1–13

'Jesus, full of the Holy Spirit, returned from the Jordan and
was led by the Spirit in the desert' (v. 1, NIV).

Luke records that, as Jesus was about to begin his public ministry, he was led, 'full of the Holy Spirit', into the desert where, for forty days, he was tempted by the devil. Those forty days were marked by physical hunger and testing that questioned the very foundations of his being. At Jesus' baptism the voice of God from heaven had said, 'You are my Son, whom I love' (3:22). In the desert Satan turned that affirmation into a taunting uncertainty, 'If you are the Son of God . . .'

St John of the Cross called this desert experience the dark night of the soul. It is a reality for most believers at some stage of their journey, and for many it happens not long after conversion. The first joy of meeting Jesus, of knowing God's forgiveness and of finding wonderful treasures in God's word gradually, or at times suddenly, seems to dissipate. What once was full of joy and certainty becomes difficult and heavy. Prayer, which once was a delight, feels more like a duty or, if we're honest, drudgery. The Bible reads like any other book. Doubt and confusion replace the things that we once felt so sure about. Worship is no longer a moving experience. Worst of all is that God seems to have taken his leave.

God has not let us down, nor abandoned us. This desert place is an important part of the journey of faith. God is like a father who teaches his son to ride a bike. At the start, the father's hand on the back of the bike helps the boy to get his balance but gradually, as the father lets go, the child learns to balance himself and in no time he can ride. At some stage of our journey God withdraws his hand so that we learn to walk by faith rather than by feelings. The desert becomes the place where we learn to endure and where we become strong.

*'In the wilderness I learned to love God truly . . . because there was nothing else left.'*

**Frederick Buechner**

# SATURDAY 15 MARCH
## When I Feel as Empty as an Autumn Tree

### Matthew 6:25–34

'If that is how God clothes the grass of the field, which is here today and tomorrow is thrown into the fire, will he not much more clothe you, O you of little faith?' (v. 30, NIV).

Hawkeye Pearce, in the TV series *MASH*, reckoned that autumn in his home-town in Crabtree Cove, Maine, was so beautiful, you'd think that God had invented new colours just for the occasion. I know what he meant. In certain parts of New Zealand, autumn is so beautiful it hurts. Trees are as glorious as an artist's palette with greens and golds mingling with reds and rusts. When the leaves fall, the carpet under the trees invites scuffing and crunching through. Then the tree stands bare and empty, silhouetted against a grey winter sky.

Autumn is the season for letting go. Like the trees, I need to let go my reds of raw hurt and anger, my greens of jealousy and envy, my yellows of fearfulness and resentment, my browns of regret and bitterness.

There are other lettings-go as well. A child leaves home, an elderly parent dies, a friendship turns sour, a prayer partner moves away, a job change puts a 'dent in my identity'. At such times, an empty autumn tree invites me to stand and gaze, to put my arms around its trunk and listen. How does it feel to lose so much, to be so empty?

How does a tree give shade when it is stripped and bare? How do I give shade to someone else when I too feel exposed and vulnerable? How can I pour out living water to another parched soul when my own well has run dry? How can I offer bread to a hungry friend when, like Mother Hubbard, my cupboard is bare?

While I find such emptiness scary, I discover, with surprise, that my letting go makes space for new life and for God's refilling. C. H. Spurgeon said, 'Empty buckets are fittest for the well of grace.' Poet Macrina Wiederkehr calls this autumn emptying the sacrament of letting go and the sacrament of waiting.

---

*Jesus,*
*You speak to me of an inner shade*
*whose name is peace*
*the gift that comes from letting go.*
        ***Seasons of Your Heart***

# SUNDAY 16 MARCH
## God Rules the World

### Psalm 82

'Rise up, O God, judge the earth, for all the nations are
your inheritance' (v. 8, NIV).

Psalm 82 is a psalm unlike any other. Using the imagery of a heavenly court in session, the psalmist describes God (*Elohim*) passing judgment on other 'gods' (*elohim*) who are presumably human leaders or officials. Their crime is that they have abused their position by not honouring their responsibilities. They have misgoverned and misled those who looked to them for justice and help. Their task was to defend the cause of the weak and fatherless and to maintain the rights of the poor and oppressed, but they have failed. They have proved themselves to be powerless, incompetent and, perhaps most damning of all, ignorant (*v. 5*).

Their personal failure has had an earthshaking effect. God thunders out his judgment, sentencing them to death. These so-called 'gods' are not identified or named. They do not speak in self-defence or in response to God's judgment. Like a dream in the night they disappear from view.

We could be tempted to write this psalm off as unusual, but Jesus himself quoted from it. In John 10:34–36 he referred to Psalm 82:6

to defend his claims to be God. If God could call these mere men gods, why was it blasphemous for him, the Son of God, to declare himself equal with God?

Jesus himself embodied the teaching of this psalm. To religious leaders who thought they knew everything about God, Jesus spoke with new and compelling images of a God who is a compassionate father with welcoming arms always open, a God who offers forgiveness far beyond deserving, a God who has special concern for the poor, the weak, the powerless. For Jesus, righteousness and justice lay at the very heart of religion.

The apostle James echoed this same theme in his description of pure and faultless religion as looking after orphans and widows in their distress, and keeping oneself from being polluted by the world (see *Jas* 1:27). Psalm 82, for all its imaginative poetry, is a pertinent reminder of that call today.

### Prayer for today
*'Your kingdom come, your will be done* **on earth *as it is in heaven' (Matt* 6:10).**

# MONDAY 17 MARCH
## When I am Led by the Vulnerable Way

Luke 13:31–35

'How often I have longed to gather your children together,
as a hen gathers her chicks under her wings' (v. 34, NIV).

If you were asked to name a saint who walked confidently in the constant sunshine of God's presence, you might well name Mother Teresa. Her work among the sick and dying of Calcutta gave the world a glimpse of a tiny woman with a huge faith in God. But letters and diaries written by Mother Teresa, which are now being published by an Indian theological journal, reveal a woman who knew the dark night of the soul at first hand.

Frequently feeling unable to pray, she encouraged her nuns to keep praying. 'This cleaving to each other, Jesus and I, is prayer,' she wrote in 1966. As she walked about the slums of Calcutta she constantly told God how much she longed for him. A friend who knew her well said that a 'lifelong night of darkness' enfolded Mother Teresa from the time she embarked on her life of service to the abandoned. At the beginning she was tempted to return to Europe, writing of 'all the beautiful things and comforts', but she resolved to remain on her mission. Even the greatest saints, it seems, come to joy not in strong, confident steps, but by the vulnerable way.

I glimpse the vulnerable beauty of a single violet growing in a patch of weeds. I find a monarch butterfly lying on the ground, its fragile wings damaged. I hear a young Afghan woman on television, educated and articulate, speaking of her work in Pakistan among refugees from her own country. She longs to go home to Afghanistan. Why? Simply because it is home. I read of Jesus weeping over Jerusalem and longing 'to gather your children together, as a hen gathers her chicks under her wings'.

In our world where strength is measured by military might and superiority, Jesus still calls his followers to live by the way of peace, of non-retaliation, of forgiveness. This God of the vulnerable way is likened, not to a keen-eyed eagle who sweeps and soars through the skies, but to a defenceless mother hen who gathers her chicks in protection beneath her wings.

# TUESDAY 18 MARCH
## When I Feel Scattered

Psalm 77:1–15

'I will remember the deeds of the LORD; yes, I will
remember your miracles of long ago' (v. 11, NIV).

'Superficiality is the curse of our age,' says author Richard Foster. 'The desperate need today is not for a greater number of intelligent people, or gifted people, but for deep people' (*Celebration of Discipline*).

There are times when I feel scattered, spread a mile wide and an inch deep. It is usually busyness and the demands of the outer journey of life that bring me to this point. But I am more than a physical being, eating, walking and sleeping. As a 'creature of sense of spirit', I am also on an inner journey. The challenge, to use Evelyn Underhill's phrase, is to learn how to live 'an amphibious life' or, as Thomas Kelly puts it, to learn to live 'concurrently', that is, making the two journeys at the same time.

One way of dealing with the feeling of being scattered is to do what the psalmist urged – 'Remember' or, to write it a little differently, 're-member', meaning to put back together again. Reflecting on God's grace-filled activity in the past, remembering how he has been faithful, perhaps drawing a time line of his leadings – these can all be ways of gathering the inner scatteredness and coming to wholeness once again.

Author Joyce Huggett tells of a woman on a prayer retreat who was asked to find a symbol of how she was feeling. She said, 'I feel scattered, like a dandelion seed head, one of those "clocks" that children blow on until all its seeds are scattered.' At the end of the retreat she used the same image, but said, 'Now all the fragments of myself have been gathered back together and I feel whole again.' As she recalled the way God had met her, she had been 're-membered', put back together again.

There will be many distractions in this day that push and pull, demanding attention and energy. In the midst of all the scatteredness, take a moment to remember some aspect of God's faithfulness in your life. As you do, you may well find yourself 're-membered' at the same time.

**To pray**
*Lord, remember me today.*

# WEDNESDAY 19 MARCH
## When My Soul is Parched

Isaiah 58:6–12

'The LORD will guide you always; he will satisfy your
needs in a sun-scorched land and will strengthen your frame.
You will be like a well-watered garden, like a spring whose
waters never fail' (v. 11, NIV).

This portion of Isaiah is full of salvation and joy. When God's people live in righteousness, sharing their food with the hungry, providing the poor wanderer with shelter, clothing the naked, then even the land bursts with blessing. Pictures of well-watered gardens and unfailing springs speak lushness and abundance.

Oh the bliss of those times when my soul's garden feels like that. Oh the sad reality when the gold seems to have lost its lustre (*Lam 4:1*), when my heart feels heavy and my soul is parched. 'Lord Jesus Christ, Son of God, have mercy,' I pray. Those dry times seem to come most often when I've just given out in some way – a seminar to organise, a workshop to conduct, an edition to complete. Every ounce of energy is focused on that task, then, when it's over, I feel like Elijah post-Carmel, slumped in exhaustion beneath a broom tree (*1 Kgs 19*).

There can be other reasons for spiritual dryness as well. Soul-neglect and busyness can squeeze the regular patterns of reflection, prayer and Bible study out of shape. A sudden crisis or circumstance may 'send the spiritual furniture of our souls spinning across the floor like deckchairs on the Titanic', as someone has put it. Some dry times have nothing to do with us at all. For unknown reasons, dust storms whip up, leaving our soul's field bare but for a few weeds.

John Newton, songwriter of 'Amazing grace', once wrote to a parishioner who found herself in a time of spiritual dryness:

Such seasons are like winds to the trees, which, by blowing them every way, loosen the ground about them, circulate the sap, and cause them to strike their roots to a greater depth, and thereby secure their standing.

In times of dryness we need to look deeper than the surface. The God who never hibernates and who is never unfaithful, is always graciously at work in our lives. Through the seasons of growth and fallow, freeze and thaw, God works the soil and strengthens the plant.

---

### To reflect on
*What waters your soul?*

83

# THURSDAY 20 MARCH
## When I Cannot Find My Way

Psalm 32:1–11

'I will instruct you and teach you in the way you should go;
I will counsel you and watch over you' (v. 8, NIV).

There are times on the Christian journey when the way forward is sunlit, clearly signposted and we can see exactly where we are going. The shimmering horizon and blue skies beckon us forward. Then there are other times! This faith journey, like any road, has its twists and turns, detours and delays. Without warning, we can be plunged into a dark valley, covered by bush and cloud. Uncertainties litter the roadside. Questions and doubts point their accusing fingers. 'Do you know where you are going?' 'Are you even on the right road?'

What do we do when the highway of our God feels more like the road to nowhere?

A local Christian paper recently told the story of a Catholic priest who returned to the priesthood after fourteen years' absence. He had taken sabbatical leave overseas but, when he returned to New Zealand, he found he was 'unable to fit the old shoes'. 'All the props were gone,' he said. 'I was quite confused. I was very aware I was on a spiritual journey but there were no signposts and I had no idea what I was going through. It was

something with no name.'

He walked through this no-man's-land of the soul, supported by colleagues and held by a lifeline of prayer. Eventually he obeyed his heart's call and returned to the priesthood. 'To go forward like a man in the dark is the meaning of this dark vocation,' said James K. Baxter.

There are times when we wish God would just give us a map showing us how to get from here to heaven, but he does not. Instead, he walks alongside us through all the twists and turns of life, his unfailing presence providing the guidance and sure strength we need to live out his purposes.

---

*Thy Word is a lamp unto my feet*
*And a light unto my path.*
*When I feel afraid, think I've lost my*
  *way*
*Still you're right there beside me.*
*And nothing will I fear as long as you*
  *are near*
*Please be near me to the end.*
    *Amy Grant and Michael W. Smith[2]*

# FRIDAY 21 MARCH
## When it is Winter in My Soul

1 Kings 17:7–16

'The jar of flour was not used up and the jug of oil did not run dry, in keeping with the word of the LORD' (v. 16, NIV).

I read about a family of children who were given some baby rabbits with soft, downy skin. The children's mother worried about what would happen to the rabbits when summer's warm days gave way to winter's snow. What she did not know was that rabbits grow fur as the temperature demands. The colder it becomes, the thicker their fur grows.

There are times when our inner resources seem almost depleted and we are thrown into winter. A child becomes ill, a teenager turns to drugs, a marriage begins to disintegrate. We feel like the widow of Zarephath who had only a handful of flour and a little oil left. We cry 'Enough' and 'What are you doing, God?' and 'I cannot handle this.'

It is true that we cannot. But our fur has not grown yet. As we plunge into the crisis, our capacity increases. A new strength, unfamiliar and untested, emerges and we wonder where it came from. Strangers become friends who stand alongside us and lend support and encouragement.

A missionary on furlough spoke of dark and testing days in his appointment. 'I had to learn to dig deeper,' he said, 'deeper into the Word, deeper into God himself, and I found a new opening at the bottom of my well.'

A friend who owned a farm in Zambia watched in dismay as a large part of her property went up in smoke. This was not at the usual time of burn-off at the end of harvest. For this woman, recently widowed and trying to make a go of the farm on her own, this unseasonable burning was devastating. A few days later, a neighbour stood with her, looking over her blackened fields and said, 'Bee, you'll be the first to have green grass.'

In those deep, dark days when, like Narnia under the spell of the White Witch, it is 'always winter and never Christmas', God may be growing green grass and thick fur in our lives.

*When we reach the end of our hoarded resources*
*Our Father's full giving is only begun.*
*Annie Johnson Flint, SASB 579*

# SATURDAY 22 MARCH
## When Prayer Seems to Go Unanswered

Matthew 7:7-11

'You may ask me for anything in my name, and I will do it'
(John 14:14, NIV).

In May 1955 a man named Bob Mitchell received a letter written by Jim Elliot who had recently moved to Ecuador with his young wife and baby daughter to pioneer a missionary outreach to the Auca Indians. The Aucas lived in a remote area and were considered hostile. In his letter, Jim mentioned that a mutual friend and partner in ministry, Ed, had already left to make contact with the tribe. With a mixture of excitement and trepidation, Jim asked Bob to pray for them, especially for Ed.

As requested, Bob prayed for his friends' protection and for the success of their ministry. But several months later those friends – Ed, Jim and three others – were murdered by members of the very tribe they were trying to reach. Bob's prayers, it seemed, had gone unanswered.

Why do such things happen? A fervent young Christian prays for guidance but fails to receive any clear sense of direction. A mother prays for her child's healing but watches as the disease takes its relentless toll. An elderly couple pray for their grandchildren's salvation, but see no results. Why do the prayers of sincere, mature believers so often seem to fall on deaf ears?

Jesus' extravagant promises make the question even more perplexing. He promised that if we ask, we will receive; if we seek, we will find; if we knock, the door will be opened (*Matt 7:7-11*). He guaranteed that if we ask anything in his name, he will do it (*John 14:14*). Jesus' promises stir an expectation within us that our prayers will be answered, and lead to perplexity and disappointment when they are not.

Years later, Bob Mitchell attended an international conference where he met a South American evangelist who was one of the very men from that Auca Indian tribe who had murdered Jim Elliot and his colleagues. When Bob heard how the Aucas had become Christians, he realised that his prayers had been answered after all.

## To reflect on
*The mystery of unanswered prayer draws us ever closer to God, who is the answer to all our prayers.*

# SUNDAY 23 MARCH
## A Prayer for God to Act

### Psalm 83

'Let them know that you, whose name is the LORD – that you
alone are the Most High over all the earth' (v. 18, NIV).

Psalm 83 brings to a close a collection of psalms ascribed to Asaph, the leader of one of David's Levitical choirs. The Asaph psalms are dominated by the theme of God's rule over the world. Words of warfare, enemies and national threat are woven together with declarations of praise and prayers for God's help. Psalm 83 reads like a history lesson but there was no actual time in Israel's history when all ten nations listed here were in alliance against Israel. The nation lived under constant threat, so the psalm would have often been a timely prayer.

The psalmist's opening plea, 'O God, do not keep silent', is for God to act. This is no time for God to hold himself aloof. Israel's crisis is God's crisis; her enemies God's enemies. The aim of the attacking nations is clearly to destroy the nation of Israel, to wipe out all memory of its name and existence (v. 4). The psalmist recalls God's saving acts and intervention in the past. Do it again, God, to all those who threaten 'the pasture-lands of God'. Make the enemies 'like tumble-weed . . . like chaff before

the wind'. This word picture recalls the description of the wicked in Psalm 1 who, 'like chaff that the wind blows away', disappear without trace. This is the unspeakable fate that her enemies want for Israel.

The psalmist makes clear, however, that the ultimate goal of God's intervention is not just the security of Israel and the destruction of her – and God's – enemies. He pleads, not for revenge, but that all the enemies of God will seek him, turning to him in penitence and acknowledging that power and glory belong to God alone.

This is great far-sighted praying, which echoes Jesus' bidding to look beyond human revenge and to 'love [and] pray for those who ill-treat you' (*Luke 6:27,28*). In a world shaken by violence, where the 'you hit me and I'll hit you back even harder' philosophy of retaliation has failed to bring peace, perhaps we can do no better today than pray for God's kingdom to come.

# MONDAY 24 MARCH
## When I Go by the Roundabout Way

Exodus 13:14–18

'When Pharaoh let the people go, God did not lead them on the
road through the Philistine country, though that was shorter.
For God said, "If they face war, they might change their minds
and return to Egypt" '(v. 17, NIV).

When the children of Israel left Egypt, heading for the promised land of Canaan, theirs was a journey from slavery to freedom, from poverty to abundance. It sounded like a straightforward journey, from cruel servitude, to 'a land flowing with milk and honey' (v. 5). The people did not expect it to be a long trip. All they had to do was cross the Sinai peninsula, which they could do in a matter of weeks. But God had an alternative route in mind.

The Bible says, 'God led the people around by the desert road toward the Red Sea' (v. 18). Instead of going north–east towards the promised land, the pillar of cloud and fire that guided them headed south. They were dismayed and confused, but God knew exactly what he was doing. The people got out of Egypt in a night, but it would take forty years to get Egypt out of them. For 400 years they had been treated like slaves, acting and thinking like slaves. The time in the desert would teach them to be the covenant people of God.

God still leads his people by a roundabout way. He is never rushed to get us from A to B, for his priority is to build Christlikeness and character within us. We pray, 'God, I need patience, and I need it in a hurry,' and God answers by putting us into a work situation or in a family where our patience is tested to the limit. We sing 'To be like Jesus', but it is only when the testing comes or the dream dies that we begin to know what it is to be like Jesus in the fellowship of his sufferings (Phil 3:10). We long for strength, but feel the overwhelming weight of our own weakness.

Jesus himself faced the roundabout way of rejection, denial and crucifixion, but his cry of abandonment (Mark 15:34) was not the last word in his life. Nor will it be in yours.

### To reflect on
*What God does in us is more important than what he does for us.*

# TUESDAY 25 MARCH
## When Sorrows Overwhelm

Isaiah 63:7–9

'In all their distress he too was distressed, and the angel of his presence saved them. In his love and mercy he redeemed them; he lifted them up and carried them all the days of old' (v. 9, NIV).

A woman I know passed through a deep valley of sorrow when her son became ill with leukemia. In spite of the best medical care, the boy died at just nine years old. My friend was devastated, her fragile faith in God shattered. Over subsequent months we met together regularly, but often just sat in silence as she coped with her overwhelming grief. She said that a large part of herself had died with her son.

Then, ever so slowly, she began to live again. She became part of a support group for parents whose children were having treatment for cancer. She undertook study in the area of counselling. She gradually picked up the shattered pieces of her life and began to assemble them in a new way. Today she is a fully qualified counsellor, working with people who are struggling to find their way through grief. When I reflect on the unfolding ministry of my friend's life, I get a glimpse of God's redemption.

Christians use the word 'redemption' to describe the work that Jesus did on the cross when he gave his life on our behalf. His death was the price he paid to buy our freedom from the penalty of sin. But redemption is more than a one-time event. It continues to happen every day as people like my friend stand alongside others in their grief and loss, and are able to say, 'I know what it's like.' Each person's grief is distinct and personal, but the sad journey through sorrow that my friend made has given her the gift of empathy with others.

God is still in the redeeming business. We may not welcome the sorrow that overwhelms us but gradually, in his time, our healing will come and, with it, the ability to stand alongside others in their heartache and say, 'Let me tell you of the One who helped me to live again.'

*Bearing my sorrows, bringing my pain,*
*Yielding my heartache, coming again.*
*Today I will trust you, have faith in you, Lord.*
*Show me your healing, Redeeming God.*

# WEDNESDAY 26 MARCH
## When I Have to Hold on by My Fingertips

Hebrews 11:1–3

'Now faith is being sure of what we hope for and certain of what we do not see' (v. 1, NIV).

I have to confess that I have no head for heights. I'm fine if I have a solid railing or someone's firm grip to hold on to, but the very thought of climbing somewhere high by myself makes my heart pound and my hands sweat. I watch a documentary on television of someone rock-climbing high in the mountains, and I marvel. Spider-like, the climber inches up a vertical rock face with scarcely anything to put his feet on and clinging by his fingertips to tiny bumps in the damp rock. There seem to be no resting places, no sight of the summit, little way forward and definitely no way back.

At times the life of faith seems just like that. Instead of an easy stroll along a pleasant path, the journey that God leads us on can bring us to desperate places where we are left in the dark, hanging on by our fingernails, as it were. Fingertip faith, it has been called. In such moments, when the way forward is hidden by dark cloud or overhanging rock, we have to hold on as if God is still with us, that his love is unchanging and that he can be trusted.

The saints who have gone before us knew about this fingertip faith. There was a time when John Wesley felt that he could no longer preach to others because of his own lack of faith. Peter Böhler, a wise pastor and friend, advised Wesley, 'Preach faith till you have it. And then, because you have it, you will preach faith' (*Journal*, Saturday 4 March 1738).

If we have known anything of God's goodness and faithfulness in the past, that is a fingerhold to cling to in the present moment. And as we do hold on, even by our fingertips, we will discover, when the clouds part and the sun shows our way forward, that in fact we have been held on to all the time.

*His love in time past*
*Forbids me to think*
*He'll leave me at last*
*In trouble to sink.*
                    **John Newton, SASB 712**

# THURSDAY 27 MARCH
## When I Feel Broken

Psalm 147:1–11

'He heals the broken-hearted and binds up their wounds' (v. 3, NIV).

I heard a woman pray recently in a church service, 'Thank you, God, for all the blessings that come out of buffetings.' 'Mmm,' I thought, 'those are not just empty words. That woman knows something of heart-ache and hurt.' If sadness was portioned out equally, which of course it is not, that woman, as the mother of a large family, has had more than her share. Yet, in a moment of prayer and reflection, she could see beyond the buffetings, as she called them, to the blessings.

In the history of God's people, there were times when the only way for God to get their attention was for him to batter and break them. In the heart of the book of Isaiah, God speaks desperate words to his obstinate people who have turned their backs on the only One who could save them. But his words of judgment are tempered by words of mercy and healing. 'You will weep no more,' he tells them. 'How gracious he will be when you cry for help!' 'The moon will shine like the sun . . . when the LORD binds up the bruises of his people and heals the wounds he inflicted' (*Isa 30:19,26*). Their brokenness was not to destroy them but to turn them

back to God, to make them realise their utter dependence upon him.

It is much the same for us – an unexpected illness, an untimely death, a reversal of fortune or reputation. God's breaking can wear many disguises as he upsets the tidy package of our lives and casts us upon his unfathomable resources. A. W. Tozer said, 'It is doubtful that God can use greatly anyone he does not hurt deeply.'

What is surprising, as we look back later, is that our deep hurt and brokenness did not signal the end of God's working in our lives but, in fact, the beginning of a new, deeper, more lasting work. As Ernest Hemingway put it, we become strong at the broken places.

---

*In the buffetings and breakings of this day, may you meet with the God of blessing.*

91

# FRIDAY 28 MARCH

## When Storms Blow

Psalm 1

'He is like a tree planted by streams of water, which yields its fruit in season and whose leaf does not wither. Whatever he does prospers' (v. 3, NIV).

Not far from the city where I live is the Akatarawa Valley, a sparsely populated area that is lush with trees. At certain times of the year, winds roar through the valley, bending and straining everything in their way. In the early years of last century, a local church was built, using wood from the rimu trees in this valley. Seventy years later, when the church was moved and enlarged, some of the original wood was stored in a shed behind the new church hall. The shed eventually deteriorated and had to be demolished, but the timber from the old church was salvaged.

A local woodturner offered to use the wood to make tables that could be sold to raise church funds. The wood was very heavy and full of large nails and bolts but, when sawn, it was found to contain some of the most beautiful heart rimu he had ever seen. 'Those winds,' he said, 'that swept through the Akatarawa Valley in the early 1900s, twisting and stressing the wood during its growth, helped to form the dark and beautiful grain of the heart-wood.' The strongest storms, it seems, create the toughest wood.

The psalmist declared that a believer who delights in the Lord and who meditates constantly on God's word is like a tree, strong and fertile. In my own life, I have not gone looking for storms or crises, but I have to admit that the most stretching times in my journey of faith have come from those experiences that shook me to the very depths of my being and forced me to send the roots of my tree-life down, down ever deeper into God. He not only allowed the storm, but was in the storm to sustain me.

---

## To reflect on

*'When the great oak is straining in the wind, the boughs drink in new beauty, and the trunk sends down a deeper root on the windward side. Only the soul that knows the mighty grief can know the mighty rapture. Sorrows come to stretch out spaces in the heart for joy.'*

**Edwin Markham**

# SATURDAY 29 MARCH

## When Prayer is Like Throwing a Gumboot

James 2:14–17

'Dear friends, do you think you'll get anywhere . . . if you learn all the right words but never do anything?' (v. 14, *The Message*).

There's a place in New Zealand that has a gumboot as its symbol, and an annual gumboot-throwing festival. Drive through the town and you're sure to see someone crossing the main street wearing gumboots. Keep an eye on your rear-vision mirror in case a practice shot comes hurtling towards you.

In my life, I've thrown wobblies, but never wellies, as gumboots are called in other places. Like discus-throwers at the Olympics, there must be a way of preparing to throw a gumboot, through a series of twirls and turns, that gathers momentum and then lets the released gumboot fly through the air with the greatest of ease, to borrow a phrase from a song about another flying object.

Gumboot-throwing reminds me of prayer. At times we struggle and wrestle with a prayer that takes shape within us, but there comes a point when we simply have to fling it out with all the strength we can muster. Unlike throwing the gumboot, however, in prayer we have to fling ourselves after it.

What good is it, asked James, if you say kind words or even pray for someone who is needy, but then do nothing about their need? What good would the Samaritan have done if he had merely spotted the beaten-up traveller on the side of the road, and stood there and had a prayer meeting for him (see *Luke 10:33*)? Prayer and participation need to be tied together, intercession and involvement.

Anthony Bloom, head of the Russian Orthodox Church, says in his book, *School for Prayer*, that 'words of prayer must also be words of commitment'. Praying for peace, we need to become peace-makers in our homes and communities. Praying for someone's healing, we need to create the conditions in which healing can occur. Anthony Bloom says, 'It is absolutely pointless to ask God for something which we ourselves are not prepared to do.'

Think about what you pray for today. 'Thy kingdom come, thy will be done . . .' Are you prepared to fling yourself, like a gumboot, after your prayer?

# SUNDAY 30 MARCH

## The Pilgrim Psalm

Psalm 84

'Blessed are those whose strength is in you, who have set their hearts on pilgrimage' (v. 5, NIV).

The great autumn festival is at hand. A long year of toil in the fields and vineyards is over and the produce of the land safely gathered in. The late–summer ground is parched and all the stream beds are dry. The autumn rains are expected any time now. The rain will soften the earth and make it ready for a new cycle of planting and growing. From every village and town come pilgrims heading towards Jerusalem. As they draw near to the temple they sing a song like this.

It is a song of longing. The pilgrims are as thirsty for God's presence as the parched ground is for showers. Coming to the temple after months of toil is like coming home after a long weary journey.

It is a song of celebration. The holy place, symbol of God's presence, is a refuge even for the common birds, sparrows and swallows, who build their nests and hatch their young in the safe, undisturbed confines of the temple. Birdsong joins with pilgrim song in praise to God.

It is a song of strength. The dry and difficult terrain through which the pilgrims pass – the Valley of Baca – has been a testing ground causing tears and heartache. But the pilgrims' tears are like the autumn rains that turn the dry valley into springs. The plants revive and cover the ground with colour and fragrance.

It is a song of sacrament. The pilgrims come, knowing that their visit to the temple will nourish and fortify them for the months ahead. One day there is worth a thousand anywhere else. Their journey becomes a means of grace, a spiritual encounter with the holy.

We are a long way in time and distance from these pilgrims. Our journey to the temple of God's presence takes us through the Valley of Busyness and Distraction. We are likely to carry more than a knapsack with some dried bread in it. But this psalm calls us to set our hearts on pilgrimage. The pilgrim songs of celebration and sacrament can be our songs as well.

# MONDAY 31 MARCH
## When I'm Feeling Unfinished

Philippians 3:10–14

'Not that I have already obtained all this, or have already been made perfect, but I press on to take hold of that for which Christ Jesus took hold of me' (v. 12, NIV).

A simple cross-stitch sampler lies in my drawer, wondering when it is going to be completed. A box of photographs taunt me with their question, 'When are you going to name us?' There's a creative gift in starting something new; there's a persevering gift in completing it.

I have another unfinished project that has been on the go for over half a century. It is a work of art in process, slowly being added to, touched up, altered, improved, stretched, polished, transformed, growing and becoming every day. That project is me, myself. That project, believer, is you too.

It began a long time ago, even before you were born. Psalm 139 says you were 'knit . . . together . . . fearfully and wonderfully made . . . woven together' in your mother's womb (v. 13–15), seen and known and loved by God. But even long before that, you were a dream in the heart of God, chosen 'before the creation of the world to be holy and blameless in his sight' (Eph 1:4).

Paul had a great story of transformation to tell. His turnaround was so remarkable, you could be tempted to think that Paul, post-Damascus Road, was totally, fully transformed. Certainly he was rearranged, reprioritised and pointed in a new direction. But for Paul, just like for you and me, there was still a great deal of pressing on and persevering to do. 'I want to know Christ,' he said, 'to be like him and to become all that he had in mind for me to be.'

In the hands of God, I can be assured that I will not be tossed aside as an unfinished project. Like Paul, I can be confident that the God who began a good work in me will carry it on to completion (*Phil 1:6*). So I press on, embracing my unfinishedness and placing myself again today in the hands of a patient, loving God.

*But I know whom I have believèd,*
*And am persuaded that he is able*
*To keep that which I've committed*
*Unto him against that day.*
*Daniel Whittle, SASB 730*

# MARK 14–16

## Introduction

Throughout Mark's Gospel, Jesus is portrayed as a man on the move, calling, healing, teaching, forgiving, confronting. Everywhere he goes, throughout Galilee and beyond, people are challenged and changed. Some respond in love and follow him, while others reject him. Over every encounter hovers the question, 'Who is this man?'

During the last days of Jesus' earthly life, the voices both for and against him sound out loud and clear. A woman's loving devotion shines brightly alongside Judas' dark betrayal. Peter declares that he will follow Jesus to the very end, but in no time is denying that he even knows him. Those who shout their 'Hosanna' welcome, within a few days are demanding Jesus' death.

These powerful last chapters of Mark's Gospel tell the story of Jesus' Passion, his anguish and loneliness in Gethsemane, his unfair trial and his cruel crucifixion. He dies, a suffering Messiah with the sins of a suffering humanity on his shoulders. Mark's story of grief does not end with Jesus' death, however. The tomb cannot hold him. In the first flush of morning light, the women come to the tomb, find it empty, and hear the angel's instruction to 'Go and tell.'

That calling lies at the heart of the gospel and reaches out to believers today. It will not let us merely observe him from a distance. It will not let us be bystanders. Jesus' death and resurrection call us out into our world to serve him in our day, beneath the sign of the cross and in the light of the empty tomb.

# TUESDAY 1 APRIL

## Tension on the Streets of Jerusalem

Mark 14:1–2

'Now the Passover and the Feast of Unleavened Bread were only two days away, and the chief priests and the teachers of the law were looking for some sly way to arrest Jesus and kill him' (v. 1, NIV).

The menacing clouds have gathered. The storm is about to break over Jesus' head. Every detail of these verses is significant – the timing, the treachery, the tension. The Passover was a celebration of Israel's inheritance. It commemorated the night when God's angel 'passed over' the Hebrew homes marked by the blood of the lamb, but killed the first-born sons in unmarked Egyptian homes. The day of Passover was followed by a seven-day festival of unleavened bread which recalled the Hebrews' hurried escape from Egypt when they baked bread without yeast, for they did not have time to wait for it to rise.

The whole festival came to be called Passover and during this week the normal population of Jerusalem swelled with thousands of pilgrims coming into the city. They came, filled with hope and expectation that the Messiah would come again to deliver Israel from its foreign oppression and economic misery.

A city crowded with pilgrims means tension for the high priests and their police force who are anxious about riots. The Jewish leaders are already in a state of agitation because of Jesus' threatening actions in the temple (see *11:15–17*) and the crowd's acclamation *(11:8–10)*. They have already decided to do away with him (*3:6; 11:18; 12:12*) for his threat to the temple and their priestly class. But because of his popularity they need to act cautiously.

Their furtive plotting is filled with irony. They do not want to seize Jesus during the Feast. They need to keep the streets peaceful. They cannot afford any disturbances at this time when the city is bulging at the seams. But these leaders are merely pawns in the hands of a much bigger plan. They may be in power but they are certainly not in control. There are divine forces at work here. Whether they like it or not, the Son of God will indeed be executed during the Feast. Far more than being the liberation of the nation of Israel from Egypt, Passover will become the celebration of God's deliverance of all humankind from its bondage to Satan and sin.

# WEDNESDAY 2 APRIL

## What a Waste!

Mark 14:3–11

'I tell you the truth, wherever the gospel is preached throughout the world, what she has done will also be told, in memory of her' (v. 9, NIV).

Between the furtive scheming of the religious leaders and the dark betrayal of Judas, Mark places the incident of a woman who comes to Jesus with a heart full of devotion and a jar full of perfume. Both the alabaster jar and the perfume are expensive. Nard, sometimes called spikenard, was made from two plants, nadala and spike. Mark reports voices muttering that it was worth 300 denarii, almost a year's wages for a day labourer. In contrast to her extravagance, Judas' act of betrayal is cold and calculating. The fragrance from the perfume will scarcely have dispersed before the clatter is heard of thirty pieces of silver being counted out into Judas' sweaty palms.

Devotion and disloyalty stand in stark contrast. One kneels in an open display of unselfconscious love. The other lurks in a quiet corner somewhere and transacts its chilling business. Judas is willing to sacrifice Jesus for money. His treachery will never be forgotten. The woman seizes her opportunity to sacrifice her precious perfume.

Her act will never be forgotten either.

We know that Judas' action was wasted. Whatever was in his mind when he agreed to hand Jesus over, whether sheer greed or the desire to force Jesus to act against the Roman rule, Judas' betrayal was futile. Within a few days, realising the horror of what he has done, he throws his blood money away, and then his life (*Matt 27:3–5*).

In contrast, the woman is rebuked for wasting something so expensive. But only she, of all Jesus' followers, really seems to understand. She knows that he is destined to die and she seizes this last opportunity to express her love. Except for a kiss from Judas in Gethsemane, Jesus receives no other expression of love from anyone else during his Passion. The pouring out of her costly perfume prepares Jesus for the pouring out of his blood on the cross. Both acts of outpouring are linked. Neither act is a waste. This is the story of good news that will be preached to all the world.

# THURSDAY 3 APRIL
## The Passover Preparations

Mark 14:12–16

'On the first day of the Feast of Unleavened Bread,
when it was customary to sacrifice the Passover lamb, Jesus' disciples
asked him, "Where do you want us to go and make preparations
for you to eat the Passover?" ' (v. 12, NIV).

On the eve of Passover, 14 Nisan, work would finish at noon and the ritual slaughter of the Passover lambs would begin around 3.00 p.m. The head of each household would bring his animal to the temple where the priests would sprinkle the blood against the base of the altar and make an offering of the fat on the altar. The animals would be dressed with their legs unbroken and the head still attached to the carcass. Worshippers would then return to their homes where the lamb would be cooked. Along with unleavened bread, wine, bitter herbs and sauce, the lamb would be eaten at a family meal in the evening, after sunset. This new day, now 15 Nisan, was called the first day of Unleavened Bread.

The disciples are anxious to make preparations for the meal. They may not fully understand yet, but there is something about this Passover that belongs to Jesus. They ask him, 'Where do *you* want us to go and make preparations for *you* to eat...?' Jesus responds, giving instructions about '*my* guest room, where *I* may eat...'

Jesus' instructions indicate either a clear foreknowledge of events or, perhaps more simply, some secret arrangements that he has already made. A man carrying a water jar would be an unusual sight, since this was normally woman's work. Finding the room is like finding the donkey for his entrance into the city (*11:1–6*). When they ask about the room, the disciples are simply to identify him as 'the Teacher'. His authority as such (see *1:22*) makes him deserving of special honour. Not surprisingly, Mark concludes, 'The disciples...found things just as Jesus had told them' (*v. 16*).

The whole scene shows Jesus' calm control of the situation. He knows quite clearly what will happen in the next few hours. We may be certain that he also knows what will happen in the next few days. The significance of Passover as a historical event is about to be transformed for all time.

## To reflect on
*'Christ, our Passover lamb, has been sacrificed' (1 Cor 5:7).*

# FRIDAY 4 APRIL
## How Could He?

### Mark 14:17–21

'While they were reclining at the table eating, he said,
"I tell you the truth, one of you will betray me – one who is
eating with me" ' (v. 18, NIV).

What was going on for Judas as he sat with Jesus and the others at the meal? Most modern paintings of the Last Supper show the disciples sitting calmly round the table. Judas can usually be identified as the dark one with shifty eyes. Mark's word-painting of the scene, however, suggests that there was a look of sadness and worry on each disciple's face. The haunting question on their minds is, 'Which one of us could possibly betray him?'

As they each take a piece of bread, or a piece of meat wrapped in bread, and dip it into the shared bowl of sauce, Jesus tells them that 'one who is eating with me' will betray him. One by one they ask, 'Surely not I?' Jesus reassures no one. He points no finger, fixes none of them with a stare. He simply gives an ambiguous response, 'It is one of the Twelve ... who dips bread into the bowl with me.'

In that culture, eating with a person was more than a social event. It was a way of saying, 'I am your friend and I will not hurt you.' It was an assurance of peace, trust and forgiveness. To betray someone

who had shared his bread (the literal meaning of 'companion') was unthinkable (see *Ps 41:9; John 13:18*). Jesus adds to the chilling moment by declaring, 'Woe to that man who betrays the Son of Man!'

We, who know the end of the story, wonder how Judas could sit there and not give himself away. Were his ears not burning in shame? How could he feed on bread and betrayal at the same moment?

*How could Judas stand so close to holy things and not feel their fire?*
*Watch miracles take place and not believe?*
*Hear words of life but forbid them entrance to his own heart?*
*Let pearls slip through his fingers like sand?*
*Eat bread in friendship and then betray his friend?*
*How could he?*

Judas remains a mystery, but the question 'How could he?' is one that I too must answer for myself.

# SATURDAY 5 APRIL

## A New Covenant

Mark 14:22–25

' "This is my blood of the covenant, which is poured out for many,"
he said to them' (v. 24, NIV).

This luminous incident is bracketed by dark, shadowy predictions of betrayal and denial. How deeply Jesus knows the hearts of his followers! What anguish he must have felt as he made one last attempt to explain what was about to happen. On so many occasions in the past his clear teaching has fallen on deaf ears. He spoke about servanthood and they squabbled about greatness. On at least three occasions he predicted his death and they tried to jolly him out of such morbid thinking. Plain talk seems not to have worked, so here Jesus speaks with symbolism. He takes the bread and wine, traditional parts of the Passover meal, and gives them new significance.

At the risk of taking liberties with the text, may I suggest that this is what may have happened? As Jesus holds up the bread, gives thanks and breaks it, does his action remind them of a recent occasion when he has done the same thing in front of a crowd of hungry people by the lake (8:1–9)? He says, 'That is what is about to happen to me. I am about to be bread broken and offered, not just for you, not just for a hungry crowd, but for all the world.'

Then he takes the cup and says, 'Do you remember seeing the Passover lambs slaughtered at the temple yesterday, and their blood sprinkled against the altar? That is what is about to happen to me. My blood will be poured out, not just for a sacrifice that must be repeated every year, but once and for all time' (see *Heb 9:26*).

He calls them to remember. 'Remember the bread that fed thousands. Remember the Passover lamb. Remember these things as you go into the next few days. They will help you to understand that my body broken like bread, and my blood poured out like wine, represent the new covenant that God makes with his people.' And with this final appeal of love, Jesus offers bread and wine to each of his disciples in turn. Even to Peter. Even to Judas.

# SUNDAY 6 APRIL

## A Prayer For Turning

Psalm 85

'Will you not revive us again, that your people may rejoice in you?'
(v. 6, NIV).

The psalmists had a vital part to play in the telling of the salvation history of God's people. Like poets and prophets, they had an ability to see with a God-given perspective. In Psalm 85 the psalmist looks back to the return of the people of Israel from their exile in Babylon. It was a time of lament and distress, shown even by the land, which had become parched and broken.

The focus of the psalmist's opening prayer is the saving action of God on behalf of his people at that time. Using strong, evocative verbs, the psalmist tells how God 'showed favour... restored fortunes... forgave iniquity... covered sins... set aside wrath... turned from anger'. This God of initiative poured out his grace upon his broken people, but now the psalmist prays, 'Restore us again.' Something has happened in the intervening period. Something has been lost; love has cooled. Like a couple whose marriage has turned cold, God's people need a new touch of his unfailing love upon them. They need to turn again, so the psalmist prays, 'Restore ... revive us again', promising God that revival will bring rejoicing to his people, and promising the people that God will bring them peace. This time their turning is towards grace and love, not away from it.

With confidence he declares that God will bless them. The psalmist uses a most beautiful image to express God's gracious dealings with his covenant people. 'Love and faithfulness meet together; righteousness and peace kiss each other' (v. 10). These poetic figures describe qualities of God, expressions of his *shalom* blessing and well-being. They meet together, embracing each other in harmony and friendship, and bringing goodness and productivity to the land.

This psalm is full of movement and powerful imagery. Turning away from sin and turning towards God always results in blessing. The psalmist calls us to such turning today.

## To reflect on

*The people of God always live by both memory of what God has done in the past, and hope for what God will do in the future.*

# MONDAY 7 APRIL

## Desertion and Denial

Mark 14:26–31

'But Peter insisted emphatically, "Even if I have to die with you,
I will never disown you." And all the others said the same'
(v. 31, NIV).

The meal is over. They sing a hymn from the Hallel Psalms (*Ps 115–118*) and then go out to the Mount of Olives, east of the city. Once again Jesus tries to warn them. He has told them what will happen to him; now he tells them what will happen to them. 'You will all fall away,' he says. The word in Greek sounds like 'scandalise', and was used in the parable of the soil (see *4:17*). Jesus predicts that all of the disciples are going to be like the rocky soil, but Peter, the Rock, will have the rockiest time of all.

They all protest, disbelieving. 'Of course we will not desert you.' Peter's voice sounds vehement, almost angry above the rest. 'You can count on me, Jesus. Even if all the others do, I won't.' 'Peter,' says Jesus, with sorrow and love mingled together. 'Today, this very night in fact, before the rooster crows twice, you will deny me three times' (*v. 30, The Message*). Peter's voice sounds even more strident as he denies the denial and pledges himself even to death. The others echo in agreement.

These dark verses show the deep loneliness of the Son of Man. At a time when he needs his closest friends to be with him, they are still unseeing. He tries to warn them but they refuse to hear, just as they have done so often in the past. In spite of all that Jesus has taught, explained and demonstrated, now at the end there is little to show for his efforts. Even this fragile group of followers will be thrown into confusion and scattered in all directions.

His quotation from Zechariah 13:7, however, shows that what happens is all in God's control. The disciples' failure will not be the end of the story. He will go ahead of them into Galilee, where he will gather them like a shepherd and lead them on. His resurrection will not only defeat the powers of death, but will also overcome human failure and give every disciple the chance to begin again.

# TUESDAY 8 APRIL
## Suffering and Sleeping in Gethsemane

Mark 14:32–42

'He returned to his disciples and found them sleeping. "Simon," he said to Peter, "are you asleep? Could you not keep watch for one hour?" ' (v. 37, NIV).

At a place on the Mount of Olives called Gethsemane, Jesus takes Peter, James and John aside from the others. Peter has just boasted that he will stand with Jesus even to death. James and John declared that they would be baptised with his baptism and drink his cup (10:38–39). Now is their moment of testing. These are the same three disciples who witnessed the raising of Jairus' daughter (5:37) and Jesus' shining transfiguration (9:2). Now they will witness his agony.

Jesus asks them to stay and keep prayerful watch with him. His sorrow and deep distress are overwhelming. Falling prostrate to the ground he prays with loud lament, calling on God as *Abba* (Daddy), that word of trustful intimacy. 'Take this cup from me,' he begs. This is the human Jesus facing the horror of the cross and the burden of bearing the sins of all the world. Is there no other way?

Jesus' anguish meets the dreadful silence of heaven. This time there is no reassuring voice, no dove, no ministering angels who come to serve him. God has already spoken.

Jesus overcomes the silence, fights off the human temptation to escape, and through prayer he bows to God's will. He must accept the nails of the cross just as he accepted the stones of the desert.

The disciples, meanwhile, have fallen asleep. No doubt physically exhausted and mentally and spiritually overwhelmed with all that is happening, they sleep through his crisis just as he slept through their crisis at sea (4:37–41). Three times he admonishes their failure to keep watch with him. Their eyes are heavy, as unseeing as they have been through much of his ministry (see 8:18). They are overtaken by the weakness of the flesh and, in Jesus' moment of greatest need, they fail him miserably.

His two sharp commands, 'Rise! Let us go!' rouse them from sleep. Startled awake, blinded by flashing lights and confused by the sudden clamour that accompanies the arrival of Judas and his thugs, they scatter in every direction, desperate to save their own lives.

# WEDNESDAY 9 APRIL

## Arrested and Abandoned

Mark 14:43–52

'Just as he was speaking, Judas, one of the Twelve, appeared. With him was a crowd armed with swords and clubs, sent from the chief priests, the teachers of the law, and the elders' (v. 43, NIV).

A crowd of ruffians, armed with swords and clubs and with Judas at their head, invades Gethsemane. They have been sent by the temple officials to arrest Jesus. Judas has given them a sign: 'The one I kiss is the man.' A kiss on the hand or cheek was a normal greeting for a respected teacher. Judas acts as though everything is normal between them as, with a warm gesture of love or at least respect, he turns his friend and teacher over to certain death. We shudder at his blatant betrayal, his insult to intimacy.

Mark records no response from Jesus. Judas vanishes into the darkness as the thugs seize their prey. In the ensuing bedlam, whether by accident or intentionally, the high priest's servant has his ear cut off. Mark's account differs from the other gospels here (see *Matt 26:51–52; Luke 22:50–51*) as he records Jesus condemning the violent action of the arresting party and then declaring that the Scriptures are being fulfilled (see *Isa 53:7–12; Zech 13:7*). The Son of Man is handed over in accordance with God's will.

The significance of the moment is lost on the mob, however. The high priests are convinced that they have the upper hand and that their clever plots, secret signs and high-powered weaponry are all signs of their superiority. But Jesus has the last word. The Scriptures are being fulfilled. God's purposes are being accomplished. Jesus has eaten with sinners, offering God's mercy and forgiveness to them (*2:15–17*). Now he will be killed by sinners, but his very death will be the means by which all sinners, even ones such as these, will be offered mercy and forgiveness.

The disciples scatter. Mark adds the detail that a young man following Jesus is grabbed by the arresting party, but struggles free. Just as an artist signs his name in the bottom corner of a painting, this may well be Mark's own signature. Seized and stripped, he escapes into the night. Jesus, likewise seized and soon stripped, will not escape but will be crucified in the darkness.

# THURSDAY 10 APRIL

## Questioned and Condemned

Mark 14:53–65

'You will see the Son of Man sitting at the right hand of the Mighty One and coming on the clouds of heaven' (v. 62, NIV).

Arrested, Jesus faces both a Jewish and a Roman trial. In these verses, Mark reports the trial that takes place before Caiaphas, who was the ruling high priest, and the Sanhedrin, the Jewish high council. The Sanhedrin was made up of chief priests, elders and teachers of the law, seventy-one members in all. Under Roman jurisdiction, the Sanhedrin had considerable authority, but they did not have the power to impose capital punishment. They could flog him, but they want far more than that. These proceedings are, therefore, an investigation, a chance to fix a charge against Jesus before he is delivered to the Roman governor for final deliberation.

A night-time trial was unusual (see *Acts 4:3–5*) and no doubt hastily convened. Having arrested him, they need to act quickly. The law allowed the condemnation of an accused person only on the evidence of two or more witnesses who agreed (see *Num 35:30*). Many offer testimony against Jesus, but their statements do not agree. Then a charge is made by certain people who testify that they heard Jesus say he would destroy 'this man-made temple and in three days will build another, not made by man'.

We, who read between the lines and know that Jesus was referring to the temple of his own body, know that this statement is indeed true. Those who use it against Jesus, however, do not understand what he means, and once again their testimony does not agree. Like the Suffering Servant (*Isa 53:7*), Jesus remains silent before his false accusers.

The high priest now takes charge and asks Jesus directly if he is the Christ, the Son of the Blessed One. His piety in using a euphemistic name of God conceals his murderous heart. Jesus replies, 'I am,' publicly accepting for the first time in the Gospel that he is the Messiah. His words give the high priest the ammunition he has been desperately wanting. 'Blasphemy!' he cries, tearing his garments to emphasise his judgment. Jesus has incriminated himself by claiming to be equal with God. He is surely worthy of death.

# FRIDAY 11 APRIL
## Denial and Despair

### Mark 14:66-72

'Immediately the rooster crowed the second time.
Then Peter remembered the word Jesus had spoken to him:
"Before the cock crows twice you will disown me three times."
And he broke down and wept' (v. 72, NIV).

While Jesus faces questioning, condemnation, mockery, blindfolding and beating, a lonely figure waits below in the courtyard. These two scenes on two levels of the palace of Caiaphas play simultaneously for they are inseparably bound together.

Peter had earlier declared that he would die with Jesus, but now he follows him at a safe distance (v. 54). While Jesus is under fire inside, Peter sits with the captors and warms himself by the fire outside. As Jesus confesses the truth of who he is, Peter denies his link with Jesus and lies to save himself. He is accused of having been 'with Jesus', but he is now 'with' the crowd, trying hard to be unnoticed and anonymous.

Peter responds to the servant girl's first inquiry with a strong retort, 'I don't know or understand what you're talking about.' The disciples have repeatedly revealed their failure to know or understand (see 8:17-18). This present failure seems the most bitter of all. Peter responds with even greater vehemence when the girl voices her suspicion to the others present, 'This fellow is one of them' (v. 69). Betrayed by his own accent, he calls down curses upon himself when they accuse him, as a Galilean, of surely being one of Jesus' men. Calling down curses was more than using just a common swear-word. He says, in effect, 'God strike me dead if I'm lying.'

Somewhere close by a rooster crows and the sound pierces Peter's heart like a sword. Jesus had told Peter that he would deny his Master three times before the cock crows twice (14:30), but Peter had boastfully declared that such a thing could never happen. In words full of anguish, Mark reports that Peter 'broke down and wept'. He does not rend his garments as the High Priest did, but he rends his heart (see Joel 2:12-13) over his shameful failure. Peter the Rock disintegrates into a pile of sand.

### To reflect on
*Peter declared that he would die for Jesus, but in fact he needed Jesus to die for him.*

# SATURDAY 12 APRIL

## Accusation and Amazement

### Mark 15:1–5

'Very early in the morning, the chief priests, with the elders,
the teachers of the law and the whole Sanhedrin, reached a decision.
They bound Jesus, led him away and handed him over to Pilate'
(v. 1, NIV).

By morning a decision has been reached. The Sanhedrin has found a way to manipulate the charges against Jesus. The basic facts are clear. First, they have no power to get rid of Jesus themselves. Second, they need to convince the Roman governor that Jesus is a threat and deserves to die. Third, a religious charge of blasphemy – Jesus declaring himself to be the Messiah – will hold no water with Pilate. Fourth, they therefore need a political charge.

Mark's version is teasingly brief, whereas Luke gives a much more detailed account of the charges they report to Pilate, namely that Jesus has been guilty of tax evasion, treason and terrorism (see *Luke 23:1–5*). Pilate is a political man, so such charges would be of very great concern to him.

Jesus is brought before Pilate with his arms bound. That in itself would suggest that he poses some threat to public safety. Pilate's question, 'Are you the king of the Jews?' is presumably in response to the Sanhedrin's report that Jesus has

claimed to be a king. Jesus chooses to answer the charge enigmatically. The NIV translation 'Yes, it is as you say' is more direct than the Greek suggests. His answer is more likely to be, 'The words are yours.'

Pilate listens as the chief priests read out other charges as well. He looks to Jesus for his response, but Jesus is silent. He refuses to defend himself, he gives no explanation, offers no plea. His silence 'amazes' Pilate who sounds as if he would be quite happy to release Jesus, knowing that there is a current of envy underlying the chief priests' actions (*v. 10*). But as governor he cannot release someone who refuses to deny such a serious charge.

For Pilate, this is just another day at the office. The man before him is just another troublesome Jew. Pilate does not see him as a person needing justice, but as a problem to be sorted. In a long line of scheming chief priests and brutal thugs, Pilate's reluctant, indifferent governing may be the greatest evil of all.

# SUNDAY 13 APRIL

## An Undivided Heart

---
Psalm 86
---

'Teach me your way, O LORD, and I will walk in your truth;
give me an undivided heart, that I may fear your name' (v. 11, NIV).

Psalm 86 is entitled 'A prayer of David'. This should not surprise us, for the psalm sounds like him. It has David's distinctive touch and style upon it. David was never afraid to tell God that he loved him, nor to confess his own need. In one breath he could declare both his devotion and his desperation. 'Guard my life, for I am devoted to you. You are my God; save your servant who trusts in you' (v. 2).

During the years of his reign as Israel's king, David's enemies were threefold. There were foreign nations who frequently pressed their attack on Israel. There were those within his own kingdom who refused to acknowledge him as the Lord's anointed. And then there were enemies within his own heart, subtle and tempting voices that lured him away from full-hearted devotion to God. 'Create in me a pure heart, O God,' he prayed in Psalm 51:10. Here he repeats his cry, 'Give me an undivided heart.'

David knew as well as any modern-day follower knows that experiences of life can easily divide, separate and scatter one's heart. Multiple allegiances, hidden agen-das, double standards, mixed motives, can make anyone, even a king, look fine on the outside, but far from fine on the inside.

A recent film on TV featured an air hostess who had a husband and son in London and another husband in Rome. She lived in two worlds, keeping her lives separate. But it was not long before parts of one world intruded into the other, until eventually both worlds crashed around her. She was a graphic example of a divided heart.

As Jesus rode into Jerusalem on this day that we celebrate as Palm Sunday, it was with his face set towards the cross, resolute, single-minded, determined to endure 'for the joy set before him' (Heb 12:2). As we journey with Jesus into this Easter week may our prayer, like David's, be for an undivided, integrated, sincere, whole heart of love for the One who bought our redemption at such great cost.

# MONDAY 14 APRIL
## Barabbas Released

---
Mark 15:6–15
---

'Wanting to satisfy the crowd, Pilate released Barabbas to them. He had Jesus flogged, and handed him over to be crucified' (v. 15, NIV).

A crowd now approaches Pilate to remind him of 'the custom at the Feast' to release a prisoner. Pilate suddenly sees his way out of an awkward situation. He suggests that 'the king of the Jews' (notice that Pilate calls Jesus that) be released. But, stirred up by the chief priests, the crowd cries out for the release of the murderer, Barabbas. Until now, the religious leaders have feared the crowds and their infatuation with Jesus (see 11:32; 12:37), but now the people are like putty in their hands.

Barabbas had been arrested for committing murder in an insurrection. He may have been a right-wing extremist fighting to deliver Israel from the hated Roman rule. Or he may simply have been a bandit, a kind of heroic Robin Hood figure who robbed rich landlords, and in that way gained the admiration and support of the impoverished common people.

Pilate puts up no argument for releasing Barabbas but surrenders his responsibility by asking the crowd, 'What shall I do, then, with the one you call the king of the Jews?' With one voice, perfectly orchestrated by the chief priests, they yell, 'Crucify him!' When Pilate asks 'Why?' they only raise the volume of their screams. The crowd's choice is ironic. Barabbas, the life-taker, will go free because Jesus, the Life-Giver, takes his place on a cross.

Still today, the way of Barabbas is the way of violence, murder and revenge that grows and spreads like poison. But the way of Jesus soaks up injustice, evil and oppression like the venom of a sting and lets loose a far more powerful force of love and forgiveness (see 1 Cor 15:55–56).

Barabbas makes no actual appearance in the story. He remains in the background. Perhaps Barabbas, whose name means 'son of Daddy' or 'son of an unnamed father', represents any one of us. John Bunyan would have called him 'Anyman'. I look at the woman who anointed Jesus' feet (14:3–9) and wish I could be like her. I look at Barabbas and tremble at the same possibility.

# TUESDAY 15 APRIL
## Scourged and Mocked

Mark 15:15–20

'Again and again they struck him on the head with a staff and spat on him. Falling on their knees, they paid homage to him' (v. 19, NIV).

If this scene in Mark's Gospel were a television documentary, it would be introduced with a warning that it contains violence and should be watched with discretion. But this is no TV documentary and needs to be read, not with discretion, but with devotion.

Mesmerised by the crowd's demands, Pilate releases Barabbas and hands Jesus over to be crucified. Scourging was a usual preliminary to crucifixion and was carried out using a whip, aptly called a scorpion, made of several strips of leather plaited with pieces of bone, lead or bronze. The victim would be bound to a post. Stroke after stroke of the whip would tear deep into the flesh, ripping it into bloody shreds.

Somehow Jesus survives this treatment and is led into the court-yard of Pilate's palace where a whole company of soldiers, about 600 men, gather to mock him. Jesus' Jewish captors had mocked him as a false Messiah. Roman soldiers now mock him as a false king. They throw an old military cloak over him, its purple colour suggesting royalty, and put a crown of thorns on his head. This may have been a clump of thorns heaped together, or it could have been thorn palm leaves woven into a wreath and then inserted with long spikes from a date palm.

With mock homage the soldiers hail Jesus as 'king of the Jews' and bow down before him. Their ridicule is probably an expression of contempt for the Jews as much as for Jesus himself, suggesting that this pitiful, weak, bleeding figure is the kind of king the Jews deserve.

Jesus stands alone. He has been anointed for burial by a woman in the home of a leper, interrogated by Pilate, stripped, scourged and now mocked by soldiers as the king of the Jews. His closest friends have betrayed, denied and deserted him. At this moment, only God can deliver him.

## To reflect on
*What kind of king is this – anointed with spit, crowned with thorns, enthroned on a cross?*

# WEDNESDAY 16 APRIL

## Just Passing by

Mark 15:21–22

'A certain man from Cyrene, Simon, the father of Alexander
and Rufus, was passing by on his way in from the country,
and they forced him to carry the cross' (v. 21, NIV).

I was just passing by, head down, minding my own,
ignoring the crowd's push and shove, the dust and noise.
I've spent a lifetime minding my own business,
keeping out of trouble's way, staying anonymous,
it's safer that way, nobody asks no questions, nobody gets told no lies.
But that tap on the shoulder changed everything.

'Hey, you,' a Roman soldier yelled in my face,
'Get your shoulder under this.'
He pointed to a cross beam, a hefty piece of wood
and a figure collapsed beneath,
another poor soul on his way to Skull Hill.
'Nah,' I said, 'I'm not going that way, I'm heading to the city.'
'Oh yes you are,' shoving his spear up against my nose. 'Move it.'

I turned and stood over the wretched man.
As I lifted the wood he lifted his face, looked at me,
and a shudder went right through me.
His face was covered in blood and sweat, distorted with agony,
but it was his eyes that grabbed me.
I've never seen eyes like that before,
full of pain but something else as well.
Was it pity? For me? Why have pity for me?
I was just passing by, minding my own.

I carried his cross that day.
Don't know why I was picked but I'll tell you this –
There's something about that cross I can still feel on my shoulders,
something about his agony became my burden that day,
something about his eyes looked right into my soul.
I've changed direction.
These days no longer passing by,
minding my own business.
Now I'm minding his.

# THURSDAY 17 APRIL
## They Crucified Him

Mark 15:23–32

'And they crucified him' (v. 24, NIV).

'They brought Jesus to ... Golgotha ... They offered him wine ... They crucified him ... They cast lots.' Who were these anonymous 'they' who killed the Son of God?

'They' were soldiers just doing their job, obeying instructions, indifferently carrying out an everyday procedure. Their offer of wine mixed with myrrh was probably not so much a compassionate attempt to relieve his pain, as a way of giving him a spurt of energy so that he would last longer and suffer more. Jesus had already been stripped of his garments, and been given purple to wear – a kingly figure mocked in humiliation. Now they take his garments once again and raffle them off at the foot of the cross. This was just one of the perks of the job.

'They' were passers-by who hurl insults at him. They taunt the feeble, exhausted figure for his claim that he would destroy the colossal temple and rebuild it in three days. 'They' were the two robbers crucified with him who heap their own anguished curses on him. 'Save yourself, and us too while you're at it!'

'They' were the chief priests and teachers of the law who watch the wrought-iron nails being driven through his wrists and heel bones. Every bang of the hammer is the sound of victory for these who have heard him, hounded him and now have him just how they want him – dead. His defeat means their triumph.

For all their mockery, these God-slayers speak truth. He is the King of the Jews, as his placard announces. He will rebuild the temple, a new community of God's people that has no walls or barriers. And he has saved others but he cannot, must not save himself. It is not nails, but the love of God that binds him to the cross. His life is given as a ransom. His body is broken and his blood poured out for many. Jesus the Messiah, the Son of God, is crucified for the sins of the world.

## To reflect on
*Who crucified him? They did. But did I as well?*

# FRIDAY 18 APRIL

## Jesus Dies

Mark 15:33–39

'With a loud cry, Jesus breathed his last' (v. 37, NIV).

Darkness covers the land like a shroud from the sixth to the ninth hour (noon until 3.00 p.m.). The darkness is a symbol of God's judgment (see *Exod 10:21–23*), a cosmic sign of mourning and death. The blanket of darkness may also suggest a new beginning, just as Jesus had predicted (*13:24*).

At the ninth hour, Jesus cries out from the cross. Mark uses the same word for 'cry' as in the opening lines of his Gospel where he reported Israel's prophecy that the voice of John the Baptist would come 'calling' in the desert to prepare the way of the Lord (*1:3*). Now the paths have been made straight, and it is Jesus who cries out. His cry of abandonment echoes the God-forsaken cry of Psalm 22, but his words are misunderstood by some of the bystanders who think he is calling for Elijah. It was commonly believed that Elijah would come in times of critical need to protect the innocent and rescue the righteous.

Someone in the crowd runs to fill a sponge with sharp wine but others stop him and mockingly declare that they are waiting for a miraculous deliverance, one final sideshow performance. With this last taunt from his onlookers, Jesus lets out a loud cry and breathes his last. The loud cry is unusual for a crucified victim who would normally die of suffocation and exhaustion.

At the moment of his death, the curtain of the temple is torn in two from top to bottom. The heavens were 'torn open' at Jesus' baptism (*1:10*). Now the temple veil that separated a holy God from a sinful people is torn apart so that 'whosoever will may come' freely into God's presence.

Throughout his ministry, Jesus' identity has been a puzzle to followers and foes alike. At his baptism a voice sounded from heaven, announcing, 'You are my Son, whom I love' (*1:11*). At his death, when the centurion, battle-hardened commander of the execution, hears Jesus' powerful cry and watches his powerless death, he cries out in recognition, 'Surely this man was the Son of God!'

# SATURDAY 19 APRIL
## Waiting near the Cross

### Mark 15:40–47

'So Joseph bought some linen cloth, took down the body, wrapped it in the linen, and placed it in a tomb cut out of rock. Then he rolled a stone against the entrance of the tomb' (v. 46, NIV).

A number of people stand near the cross that day, watching and waiting. A small group of grieving women contemplates the scene from a distance. This may have been for the discreet reason of not gazing on Jesus' nakedness. Their distance may also be symbolic of their powerlessness at this present moment to help their beloved friend in any way. As women they could not speak to the Sanhedrin in Jesus' defence. They could not appeal to Pilate. They could not stand against the crowd's cry for Jesus' death. They could not overpower the Roman guards.

In Galilee, Mark reports, they had cared for Jesus' needs. Within a few hours they will be preparing burial spices to wrap around his body. But for these torturous hours as Jesus dies on the cross, they can do nothing but stand and contemplate, watch and wait and weep.

Also in the crowd that day is a man by the name of Joseph of Arimathea, obviously a pious man, whom Mark describes as 'a prominent member of the Council'. Just as a stranger, Simon from Cyrene, had carried Jesus' cross for his execution, now another stranger takes his body down from the cross for his burial. This is a bold act on Joseph's part. To ask for the body of someone executed for high treason could be looked upon as sympathising and could earn one the same fate. But as a member of the Council who condemned Jesus to death, Joseph would be above suspicion.

Pilate's only concern is that Jesus is already dead and the centurion in charge confirms this. Jesus' quick death surprises Pilate who gives permission for Joseph to remove the body. He must act quickly, for sundown is fast approaching (see *Deut 21:23*). Presumably with the help of servants, Joseph wraps Jesus' body in a newly bought linen cloth and buries him in a tomb carved in rock.

Devotion mingles with indifference in this scene. The women contemplate. The centurion confirms. Joseph collects the body and carries out the burial with dignity. Pilate couldn't care less.

# SUNDAY 20 APRIL
## He Has Risen!

Mark 16:1–6

' "Don't be alarmed," he said. "You are looking for Jesus the Nazarene, who was crucified. He has risen! He is not here. See the place where they laid him" ' (v. 6, NIV).

Mark's narrative of Jesus' Passion began with a woman who lovingly and lavishly anoints Jesus, as he interprets it, in preparation for his burial (14:8). It ends with devoted women who come to anoint Jesus after his burial. Drawn to the tomb by loyalty, they come to offer one last act of loving service to their Master and friend.

Mark's careful recording of the time explains why the women do not come sooner. They cannot purchase spices or travel about on the Sabbath, but as soon as they can, just after sunrise on the first day of the week, they come. Since those heavy hours of standing by the cross, their hands have kept busy with the preparation of the special burial spices. Such busyness may have helped to deal with the mind-numbing grief of watching Jesus die.

As they come in the crisp early morning to anoint Jesus' body, they suddenly remember the heavy stone which, slipped into its groove at the entrance to the tomb, will be impossible to shift. But to their surprise, when they arrive at the tomb they find the stone already rolled away. Curiosity mingles with caution as they enter and find a young man dressed in a white robe. He is an angelic figure who gives a typical angelic reassurance, 'Don't be alarmed. You are looking for Jesus . . . who was crucified. He has risen! He is not here.'

Those words echo around the cold and empty burial chamber. They echo in the hearts of the women who cannot speak for a whole range of emotions. Mark records that they were 'trembling . . . bewildered . . . afraid'. But what their minds cannot yet process their eyes can see, that indeed he is not there.

Those words, 'He is risen!' echo around the world today. In Salvation Army citadels, in cells, churches and cathedrals, the resurrection news is proclaimed. Jesus has not been held by death. His resurrection reverses the humiliation and degradation of his scandalous crucifixion. He is gloriously, wildly alive. A hopeless end has been transformed into an endless hope!

*Hallelujah!*

# MONDAY 21 APRIL

## Go and Tell

Mark 16:7–8

'But go, tell his disciples and Peter, "He is going ahead of you into Galilee. There you will see him, just as he told you" ' (v. 7, NIV).

Throughout Mark's Gospel, Jesus has been a man on the move, always calm and in control, but never still. That does not change after the resurrection. He is not in the tomb for the women to cling to. A joyful reunion with the risen Jesus would be like a happy–ever–after ending to the story. But the resurrection is not the end, merely the beginning of the gospel that must be proclaimed throughout the world.

The angel's greeting assures the women they are at the right tomb, 'See the place where they laid him.' The angel also identifies the one they seek as 'Jesus the Nazarene, the crucified and risen one'. He tells them that they must go to the disciples, who must in turn go to Galilee. This command is the first time that Jesus' followers are told to tell something about him. The crucifixion and resurrection mark a turning point. There is no need for silence and secrets now (see 9:9). The secret is out, Jesus is alive and is to be shared with all the world!

Peter gets special mention in the angel's message. Peter is the first and last disciple featured in Mark's Gospel (1:16; 16:7). The angel's specific mention of his name hints at Peter's full restoration in spite of his tragic failure. Jesus does not give up on his disciples, no matter how great the failure, no matter how grievous the faults.

There are other parallels between the opening and the closing of Mark's Gospel. It began with God's messenger announcing what God was about to do (1:2–8). It closes with God's messenger announcing what God has done. In the opening scene, John comes to prepare the way for the Lord. In the last scene, the way has been prepared and the disciples are to follow to Galilee, where Jesus has gone before them.

The angel's message in this closing chapter, however, is more momentous than that of the prophet. John came to prepare. The angel explains the meaning of the empty tomb and commissions the women for their new quest – to go and proclaim.

# TUESDAY 22 APRIL
## What Was that about Galilee?

Mark 16:7–8

'But go, tell his disciples and Peter, "He is going ahead of you into Galilee. There you will see him, just as he told you" ' (v. 7, NIV).

The angel speaks only a few sentences to the startled women, but his words are significant. As they leave the tomb, 'trembling and bewildered', the women may well have gone over the details again. 'Peter... What did he say about Peter? And Galilee... What was that about Galilee?'

Indeed, what was that about Galilee? The reference may simply be geographical, but there may also be a theological significance. Mark reported Jesus earlier telling his disciples that, after he had risen, he would go ahead of them to Galilee (14:28). The command now given makes one thing clear. Jerusalem, for so long believed to be the city of God and the place where he dwelt, is no longer the centre of God's activity. Jerusalem has become the city of the fruitless and condemned temple, the stronghold of hostility to the gospel, and the place of Jesus' cruel execution.

The disciples' future lies in a new location. Throughout the Gospel, Galilee has been the place of calling, faith, compassion, healing power and authority. By going back to Galilee where Jesus will be, the disciples go back to the promising birth of their first calling. There they can regroup and begin their journey of discipleship once more.

The angel's announcement that Jesus is going ahead of them does not mean that he departed a few hours before they did. The verb is used for leading troops forward. Earlier, Jesus linked his promise to go before them to Galilee with the image of shepherd (14:27–28). Now as the risen Lord, he will go ahead of them, regathering the flock that was scattered when he was crucified, and leading his Church forward.

'There you will see him,' promises the angel. For so long these fragile followers have been unseeing, unhearing, slow to understand. Now they will see him physically, but also with spiritual perception, at last understanding who he is, what his life and death mean, and how they must follow him now.

## To reflect on
*Sometimes in order to go forward, we first have to go back. Where is your Galilee today?*

# WEDNESDAY 23 APRIL
## An Unending Story

Mark 16:8

'Trembling and bewildered, the women went out and fled from the tomb. They said nothing to anyone, because they were afraid' (v. 8, NIV).

This verse marks the end of the earliest and most reliable manuscripts of Mark's Gospel. Such an abrupt ending is perplexing. After the explosive hope of the resurrection morning and the bright promise of the empty tomb, it seems an anticlimax, if not abject failure, that the Gospel ends on such a note of bewilderment and fear. The women leave the tomb, struck dumb. In spite of all they have seen and heard, Mark reports that 'they said nothing to anyone'.

It could be that the news of Jesus' resurrection from the dead is so astounding that the women simply cannot grasp it all, and need time to collect their thoughts. Such a reaction would not be unusual. Think of the disciples when Jesus calmed the storm (4:41), the Gerasenes when Jesus drove the legion of demons out of the man (5:15), or the woman with the bleeding who crept through the crowd to touch his garment (5:33). The women's silence at this overwhelming act of God is not permanent. It will only be for a time.

Could it be in fact that Mark has done something quite skilful in ending his Gospel in this way? Somehow the incompleteness draws us, as modern-day readers and disciples, into the story. Jesus promised that they would be scattered and that he would go before them to Galilee (14:27,28). We have watched the scattering with our own eyes, as it were, so we can trust that the other part of the promise will happen. With faith we imagine Jesus waiting in Galilee for his followers to come and meet him there. Will we too, who want to see Jesus for ourselves, go to where he leads – to Galilee, back to the beginning, the place of our first calling?

Just as the tomb cannot contain Jesus, neither can Mark's Gospel. The resurrection sets in motion a new story that is not yet finished or resolved. It will not be fully completed until the elect are gathered from the ends of the earth (13:27). As modern-day believers, we are the next chapter.

# THURSDAY 24 APRIL
## First-Hand Faith

Mark 16:9–13

'When they heard that Jesus was alive and that she had seen him,
they did not believe it' (v. 11, NIV).

Scholars who have studied the different style of this longer ending of Mark's Gospel believe that it may have been written by a later scribe, anxious to bring the story to a more satisfying conclusion. But if by 'more satisfying' we mean happy-ever-after and celebrations all round, then we will be disappointed. Mark's ending had the women fleeing from the tomb in bewilderment and fear. These verses speak of a dark blanket of disbelief that shrouded the believers.

When Jesus appeared to Mary Magdalene, she is reported as going and sharing the news with those who were 'mourning and weeping'. But 'they did not believe it'. Likewise, when he appeared to two walking in the country, they returned and reported to the others what they had seen and 'they did not believe them either'. Why this slowness to believe when the evidence must be so explosively clear?

Could it be simply because the resurrection and all that it meant was such a reversal of everything the followers had seen and experienced? Certainly they had heard Jesus' predictions about rising from the dead, but they had also seen him suffer, watched him die, heard that he was buried. Now to hear a report from a woman or a couple from the country that he is alive is, in a true sense, simply unbelievable.

Maybe, like Thomas, they needed to see for themselves. Or like the neighbours who told the woman at the well, once they too had met Jesus, 'We no longer believe just because of what you said; now we have heard for ourselves, and we know that this man really is the Saviour of the world' (John 4:42). Even Job said, 'My ears had heard of you, but now my eyes have seen you' (Job 42:5).

Faith – to be real, lasting, life-transforming faith – must be more than someone else's report. It must always be claimed and owned, a first-hand faith that is individual and personal. Our call is not 'Let me inform you about Jesus' so much as 'Let me introduce you to him'.

*May God help us!*

# FRIDAY 25 APRIL
## Living with Ambiguity

Mark 16:14–18

'Later Jesus appeared to the Eleven as they were eating; he rebuked them for their lack of faith and their stubborn refusal to believe those who had seen him after he had risen' (v. 14, NIV).

The longer ending to Mark's Gospel contains elements of the resurrection appearances reported in the other Gospels. John tells of Mary Magdalene, alone and weeping at the empty tomb (20:11). Two angels speak to her and then she turns and sees Jesus himself, but thinks he is the gardener. It is only when he speaks her name, 'Mary', that she recognises him.

Luke tells of the couple who are on their way to Emmaus, their hearts heavy, their minds and conversation filled with bitter 'if onlys' (24:13). They mistake the risen Jesus for a stranger and their eyes are opened only as Jesus breaks bread with them. Matthew reports Jesus appearing to the eleven disciples in Galilee, who see and worship him, but some still doubt (28:17).

The twins of faith and failure, confidence and confusion, stand together in each writer's account and in Mark's longer ending as well. Through his Gospel, these two contrasts have appeared and reappeared, and it is clear that the resurrection of Jesus does little to change the cloudy vision or the fragile confidence of his closest followers. They still waver, belief is still a struggle, courageous conviction is still just beyond reach.

It is no different for us. In this time of the 'already but not yet' of the gospel, while believers celebrate Jesus' first coming and await his second, we too live with ambiguity. We long to be strong and confident, but so often feel vulnerable and fragile. The treasure of God's life is most surely carried in the clay vessel of our humanity (2 Cor 4:7). The light of the glory of God seems to shine most powerfully through our brokenness. We cry out for strength, but God commends weakness. It is the same struggle that Paul faced: 'I delight in weaknesses, in insults, in hardships, in persecutions, in difficulties. For when I am weak, then I am strong' (2 Cor 12:10).

Only at the end of time, when the Son of Man comes again in all his glory, will all ambiguity be eliminated. Until then, we live with the mystery.

# SATURDAY 26 APRIL
## Let Loose

---
### Mark 16:19–20
---

'After the Lord Jesus had spoken to them, he was taken up into heaven and he sat at the right hand of God' (v. 19, NIV).

These last verses form a bridge between the end of Mark's Gospel and the beginning of the Acts of the Apostles. There, in the first chapter, we read of the resurrected Jesus being taken up to heaven (1:9). Jesus' ascension was his day of Mission Accomplished, the celebration of the completion of his earthly ministry. As his task came to a conclusion, the disciples' task was just beginning. Mark reports that 'the disciples went out and preached everywhere, and the Lord worked with them and confirmed his word by the signs that accompanied it'. It was both a human task (they went and preached), and a divine task (the Lord worked and confirmed). Acts will tell the story more fully of how the disciples waited and prayed until the Holy Spirit came, filling them and giving power for service.

This great message of the gospel cannot be contained. Mark's Gospel could not contain the whole story. The tomb could not contain Jesus. The message cannot be contained in a one-hour slot on a Sunday morning. The gospel has been let loose on the world, and, wherever it touches people, lives are changed.

Over the centuries, God's messengers have been persecuted, punished and imprisoned, but the message continues to be proclaimed. The messenger may be muzzled, but the message still goes forth. Stifled but never silenced, stomped on but never stamped out. The grain of wheat dies, but a new head of wheat grows and multiplies. The Christian witness of a family may die out in one generation but it leaps forth in the next or the next.

What Jesus began in Galilee, the disciples continued in Jerusalem, Judea and Samaria (*Acts 1:8*), and the Holy Spirit took to the ends of the earth. The water of life has become an unstoppable flood, which sweeps believers today into its flow. You and I have a part to play in telling and living the message of the resurrected Jesus, just as important as that of the first disciples. The Gospel of Mark is completed. The Gospel according to you has begun.

# SUNDAY 27 APRIL
## Glorious Things of Thee are Spoken

Psalm 87

'I will record Rahab and Babylon among those who acknowledge me
– Philistia too, and Tyre, along with Cush – and will say,
"This one was born in Zion" ' (v. 4, NIV).

In certain parts of the West Coast of the South Island of New Zealand, the people are fiercely parochial. Anyone who has lived all their life in the area is considered a 'Coaster', but someone moving into the district from outside can find it very hard to be accepted. I heard of a woman who lived on the Coast for more than eighty years. At her funeral service, when it was mentioned that she had arrived in the district as a three-week-old baby, someone was heard to mutter, 'I knew she wasn't a real Coaster!'

Psalm 87 has something of that flavour of honour and acceptance for those who have been born in Zion (Jerusalem). But this refers to more than the names listed on the birth register at the Jerusalem City Council. The psalm has a larger perspective, promising blessing for all who, through faith in God, declare themselves to be citizens of Zion.

The vision of Psalm 87 is that one day Jerusalem will be the spiritual centre of the whole world. She will be like a 'mother city' into which even the Gentile nations –

Rahab (that is, Egypt), Babylon, Philistia, Tyre and Cush, Israel's great enemies – will be brought through conversion, in universal worship of God. Their names will be listed in God's royal register and they will have the same privileges, benefits and security as those who are native-born citizens.

Jerusalem may sound a long way away but, like the Gentile nations listed here, we too, through faith in Christ, are 'no longer foreigners and aliens, but fellow-citizens with God's people and members of God's household' (*Eph 2:19*). By God's grace, we too are children of Zion.

---

*Saviour, if of Zion's city*
  *I through grace a member am,*
*Let the world deride or pity,*
  *I will glory in thy name.*
*Fading is the worldling's pleasure,*
  *All his boasted pomp and show;*
*Solid joys and lasting treasure*
  *None but Zion's children know.*
        ***John Newton, SASB 157***

# MONDAY 28 APRIL

## From Death to Life

2 Corinthians 5:17–21

'Therefore, if anyone is in Christ, he is a new creation; the old has gone, the new has come!' (v. 17, NIV).

What does it mean, then, to be a person of the resurrection? To live this side of Easter Sunday? To know 'the power of [Christ's] resurrection', as Paul puts it (*Phil 3:10*)? Are there people in this post–modern day who can be described in resurrection terms?

I know a young man who declares himself to be a modern–day John Newton. He was never a slave trader, but says that he certainly traded in human misery. Drugs were his game. Drugs were also the slippery slope into his own sad life of alcoholism and addiction. His story contains the usual tragic elements – heavy drinking and smoking leading to broken relationships, and eventually a suicide attempt. His rifle was at hand, but where were the bullets?

Desperate to find a way out, he rang Alcoholics Anonymous. 'I stopped drinking, but I was still addicted, so I "did a geographical".' That meant leaving town to go somewhere else, anywhere else, but he took his addiction with him. Through a series of encounters that can be explained only in God-terms, he came to the Salvation Army Bridge Programme where he found sobriety and peace with God at the same time.

At that point, his story begins to sound like that of Lazarus (*John 11*). From death to life, from darkness to light, the contrast was as real as that. 'Everything from my previous life was stripped away. Even the car that I used to carry firearms and drugs was stolen a few weeks after I was converted.' Anything he owned was sold to pay off debts. He was left with nothing and yet, with God on his side, he had everything, plus a new beginning.

These days the old games are over. Now married, he serves God in full–time ministry to those who are addicted as he once was. While the old life is gone, it seems that God, in his grace–filled economy, has not wasted a thing.

### To sing

*I am a new creation, no more in condemnation*
*Here in the grace of God I stand.*

*Dave Bilbrough*[3]

# TUESDAY 29 APRIL

## I Have a Destiny

2 Timothy 1:8–12

'I am not ashamed, because I know whom I have believed,
and am convinced that he is able to guard what I have entrusted
to him for that day' (v. 12, NIV).

A friend of mine is a woman of prayer. She talks to God and he talks to her. But one of her prayers had to wait almost twenty years for an answer. 'That's only a blink for God,' she says, 'but for me it seemed for ever.'

One of her daughters, whom I'll call Kay, was a beautiful, tender-hearted youngster. But in her teens, Kay rebelled against all that her Salvation Army officer parents stood for. One Sunday Kay threw a really bad 'teenage wobbly' and her mother went, heavy-hearted, to the morning meeting. During the service, the above passage of Scripture was read, and God said, 'That's my promise for Kay's salvation.' My friend clung to that promise as her daughter continued to rebel.

Nineteen years later, a change of appointment brought her parents to the city where Kay was living, now married. 'There was a new softness about her,' says her mother, 'but she was still away from the Lord.' One day, feeling anxious, my friend reminded God of his promise regarding Kay's salvation, and God reassured her that he is 'faithful to all his promises' (Ps 145:13).

Then Kay became unwell with panic attacks and seizures. The medical diagnosis – 'mature epilepsy'. Following one particularly bad seizure, Kay was rushed to hospital where, she told her mother later, 'I knew that if I had died, I would not have gone to heaven.' Together they prayed and Kay was wonderfully saved.

Some weeks later, tests revealed the presence of a deadly brain tumour and Kay was given only weeks to live. Her mother describes that time, which stretched out to eight months, as a mixture of anguish and awe as Kay became physically weak, but spiritually strong and radiant with God's love. Her life was transformed from darkness to light. Her testimony had a far-reaching impact on family and friends. 'I have a destiny,' she sang. Even in illness, she had a God-given work to do. Long before she died, Kay discovered that resurrection life begins this side of heaven.

## To reflect on
*Has it begun for you?*

# WEDNESDAY 30 APRIL

## Springtime's Song

Psalm 98:1–9

'Shout for joy to the LORD, all the earth, burst into jubilant song with music' (v. 4, NIV).

Resurrection is the springtime of the spirit. No matter what dress the world of nature wears, God's springtime can happen at any season of the year.

A young couple start attending a church and tell their story to a warm-hearted woman who welcomes them. 'I've been a bad husband,' he says. 'But I became a Christian a few weeks ago, and my wife is giving me a new chance.' Signs of spring.

A man hitch-hikes to a part of the country where no one knows him. 'I wanted to make a new beginning,' he says. 'I happened to walk past a church and heard singing.' He goes in and finds a group of people at prayer. Reminded of his grandmother who used to pray for him, he asks if he can stay and learn how to pray for himself now. Signs of spring.

Major Kathryn Cox, an American Salvation Army officer, tells of visiting a woman prisoner who was known as a hardened, unrepentant criminal. Rosie was serving a ninety-nine-year sentence with no hope of parole. As the cell door clanged shut behind her, Kathryn could just make out Rosie's shadow across the dark, smoky room. She spoke softly, saying, 'Rosie, I've come to tell you that I love you, and to tell you about Jesus who loves you.'

For a moment there was no response, and then Rosie began to weep silently, then to sob. As Kathryn held her, she spoke words of hope and promise from Scripture, and then a word that was God's inspiration. 'Rose, the Lord will make you bloom again.' Rosie's tears of pain became tears of repentance and healing as Kathryn prayed for her. A month later, when Kathryn visited the prison again, she found Rosie no longer in solitary confinement, no longer hostile, but blooming. Signs of spring.

---

*Teach me, Jesus, how to move with you,*
*step by step, in your love dance.*
*Touch my fears with your melting*
  *song.*
*Gift me with your laughter,*
*and, in the mystery of your Springtime,*
*show me the truth of the blossoming*
  *Cross.*

*Joy Cowley[4]*

# NOTES

1   William and Gloria Gaither, 'Shackled by a heavy burden', copyright
    © 1971 Gaither Music Company/Kingsway Music, tym@kingsway.co.uk,
    for the Uk & Ireland. Used by permission.
2   Amy Grant and Michael W. Smith, 'Thy word is a lamp', copyright
    © 1984 Meadowgreen Music/EMI Christian Music Publishing/Word
    Music, Inc. Administered by Copycare, PO Box 77, Hailsham, BN27 3EF,
    UK, music@copycare.com. Used by permission.
3   Dave Bilbrough, 'I am a new creation', copyright © 1983 Thankyou
    Music. Administered by worshiptogether.com songs excluding UK &
    Europe, administered by Kingsway Music, tym@kingsway.co.uk. Used
    by permission.
4   Joy Cowley, 'Springtime Jesus', taken from *Aotearoa Psalms*, published by
    and copyright © Catholic Supplies (N.Z.) Ltd, 80 Adelaide Road,
    Newtown, Wellington, New Zealand. Used by permission.

# INDEX

## (as from: Advent 1997)

*Words of Life* Bible reading notes
are published three times a year:

**Easter**
(January–April)

**Pentecost**
(May–August)

**Advent**
(September–December)

In each edition you will find:

- informative commentary
- a wide variety of Bible passages
- topics for praise and prayer
- points to ponder
- cross references for further study

Why not place a regular order for *Words of Life*?
Collect each volume and build a lasting resource
for personal or group study.

If you would like to contact Barbara Sampson,
her e-mail address is:

barbara_sampson@nzf.salvationarmy.org